WITHDRAWN

Extraordinary Answers to Finding
Love, Destiny & Balance in Your Life

## About the Author

Cyndi Dale is internationally recognized as an authority on subtle energy anatomy. She is the author of several books on energy healing, including the original and revised *New Chakra Healing* (now called *The Complete Book of Chakra Healing*), which has been published in more than ten languages, and six other best-selling books on the topic, including *Advanced Chakra Healing, Illuminating the Afterlife,* and *The Subtle Body.* Through her company, Essential Energy, she provides intuitive assessments and life-issues healing for thousands of clients a year, seeking always to uplift and inspire others to their true purpose and personalities. Her enthusiasm and care ignite all who attend her workshops, training sessions, and college classes, which are offered around the world.

Cyndi has studied cross-cultural healing and energy systems and has led instructional classes in many countries, including Peru, Costa Rica, Venezuela, Japan, Belize, Mexico, Morocco, Russia, and across Europe, as well as among the Lakota people and the Hawaiian kahunas. She currently lives in Minneapolis, Minnesota, with her two sons and (at last count) five pets. More information about Cyndi's classes and products is available at www.cyndidale.com.

Extraordinary Answers to Finding
Love, Destiny & Balance in Your Life

# Everyday
# Clairvoyant

# Cyndi Dale

LLEWELLYN PUBLICATIONS
*Woodbury, Minnesota*

FIRST EDITION
First Printing, 2010

Book design by Rebecca Zins
Cover design by Lisa Novak
Cover image © Digital Vision Ltd. / SuperStock

Llewellyn is a registered trademark of Llewellyn Worldwide, Ltd.

**Library of Congress Cataloging-in-Publication Data**
Dale, Cyndi.
  Everyday clairvoyant : extraordinary answers to finding love, destiny
& balance in your life / by Cyndi Dale.—1st ed.
    p.  cm.
  ISBN 978-0-7387-1923-8
  1. Clairvoyance. 2.  Life—Miscellanea.  I. Title.
  BF1325.D35 2010
  133.8—dc22

                                                2009045203

Llewellyn Worldwide does not participate in, endorse, or have any authority or responsibility concerning private business transactions between our authors and the public.

All mail addressed to the author is forwarded, but the publisher cannot, unless specifically instructed by the author, give out an address or phone number.

Any Internet references contained in this work are current at publication time, but the publisher cannot guarantee that a specific location will continue to be maintained. Please refer to the publisher's website for links to authors' websites and other sources.

Llewellyn Publications
A Division of Llewellyn Worldwide, Ltd.
2143 Wooddale Drive
Woodbury, MN 55125-2989
www.llewellyn.com

Printed in the United States of America

# Contents

**WE ARE SPIRITUAL** beings
having a physical experience.

—Pierre Teilhard de Chardin

# Introduction

You are special.

I am special.

We are each on this planet at this time to perform a service that no one else can possibly do. My service, however, does not have a tidy job description.

I am a clairvoyant. This means I see pictures—usually inside my head, but also with my physical eyes—that tell me things. People consult me to ask for pictures that relate to their own lives: to the relationship, work, and health concerns that press upon them. Most of the images are helpful. They are almost always accurate. And sometimes, they aren't very comfortable.

If I were to look at you with my Sight, I might perceive what you ate for breakfast, see colors explaining your true gifts and the work you are here to accomplish, or distinguish symbols telling me if you are happy, sad, or ill. I might visualize images or symbols that explain why you have relationship challenges, never feel loved, or have bad dreams at night. I might even glimpse your future and be able to describe what your life might be like in five years.

I prepare for work like everyone else. I get up and immediately wish I were back in bed. As soon as the companion-animal family detects the tiniest noise from me, I am petitioned to feed each one: the guinea pig, the turtle, the cat, and the two dogs. Then there's my ten-year-old son, Gabriel, who never wants to get up either. I somehow discover the wherewithal necessary to prod him out the door, step by step, pretending that good mothering includes okaying an outfit with mismatched socks (I bet you have a clothes-dryer monster, too) and homework that's only a little dog-chewed, and we stop at the local coffee shop for a muffin-and-milk breakfast. Maybe then I call my twenty-one-year-old college student, Michael, who only answers if he needs money. And all this while battling the forces of nature that label me an "enduring Minnesotan," meaning I'm Norwegian-Lutheran enough to ignore six-foot snowdrifts and mosquitoes that can pick up rodents. Doesn't this—more or less—sound a bit like your average day?

It's my workday that departs from the norm. My professional expertise involves looking energetically at other people's lives. I am asked to see pictures—not via computerized graphics, technological mediums, photographs, or some other typical means of visualization—that provide insights, solutions to problems, and glimpses into the future. I'm asked to see images of people, places, time periods, illnesses, and solutions that don't really exist until I perceive them. I'm asked to answer the questions that we all think but seldom ask—unless, that is, you sit in front of someone like me. Most of all, I'm asked to see hope.

What kinds of concerns do I hear on an average day? *My daughter was just diagnosed with cancer. My mother is dying. There has been a car accident. I lost my job. My husband caught me having an affair. My husband is having an affair. I am so depressed I can't get out of bed. I think there's a ghost in my house. I'm plagued with a curse.*

*What should I do?*

Acute concerns are often padded or accompanied by those about day-to-day life. *I hate my job; what should I do? What am I here on this earth to do? I have been fighting with my spouse a lot. I am sick; can I get well? How do I get rid of the ants in my kitchen? Do I have a soul mate? Will I ever win the lottery?* It is not unusual to have these questions; what's unusual is that my job is to answer them.

Though these questions can be asked of many different types of people, I receive them all. I am asked *all* types of questions, categorically organized here into queries about relationship and love, work and purpose, and health and balance. I consider these the three spheres of life that comprise the real meaning of being alive: the increasing awareness and experience of divine joy in our everyday lives.

There is no permanent record of the questions I am asked or the answers I provide. That's why I'm writing this book. I want you to know that you have legitimate questions and that no matter how obsolete, insignificant, embarrassing, grand, or weird they might seem, they *are* relevant and important.

Your individual questions are important. Your life is important. *You* are important. That's why I've organized Part II, the majority of this book, into three main sections, each of which deals with one of the three main spheres of life. Each section is presented in a question-and-answer format so you can imagine yourself asking a question—and receiving an answer—just as if you're on the phone with me or sitting in my office.

In this book, I also share stories from my childhood. Some may sound fantastical, but they are true. How many people can say they held tea parties with the angels when they were children? I did. I also believe that many of us did. I think many of us, as children, lived in a world inhabited by angels, demons, fairies, and spirits, caught between the realms of the living and dead. Maybe we've forgotten. Maybe we were told so many times that we were making it up that we started to believe the naysayers were telling the truth. Whatever the case, I hope my stories help you remember not just who you *were*, but who you *are*.

You are a person who dwells in a kaleidoscope of color, energy, and spirits that instruct, cajole, inform, and heal. We all live in this realm, whether we know it or not. While some can't touch this world with a wish, I can—and do.

As a child, I literally peered into the spiritual and energetic dimensions that surround us all. I was mainly enthralled with the colors and shapes around people. Over time, I came to realize that these colors had meaning, depicting others' feelings, desires, and personality traits. Some of the shapes were geometric and indicated thoughts and beliefs. Others were actually animate and described spirits and entities. I gauged others' needs and potential actions against these colors and forms, becoming an "energy codependent" at an early age. If Mom was red, I would hightail it to my room, assured that her anger would erupt soon. If my sister took on a strange cast of yellow-brown, I covered my tracks; I was about to be tattled on.

As I matured, I realized that there was a set of colors that appeared consistently, person to person. The hip area is occupied by red; the stomach is yellow. Most people have glowing halos of white (okay, more than a few exhibit a lackluster gray) shining around their heads. Bands of energy, starting with red and pulsing outward to a clear white, emanate from the skin. It wasn't until I was in my early twenties that I figured out I was perceiving an actual system, one that had been well documented for thousands of years in various cultures around the world.

I was seeing subtle energies and the energetic anatomy. Primarily, I was able to perceive the chakras and auric field. Chakras are energy organs that transfer psychic information into physical energy and back again. From childhood onward, I could perceive twelve of these energy centers in and around the body. Each performed a different set of tasks, and I grew fascinated with the insights I gleaned when viewing them. The auric field is a corresponding set of colored energies that encircle the body. As do the chakras, each serves a particular function, albeit in relation to the external rather than internal world of self.

The accuracy of my psychic awareness was first validated when I was traveling during my early twenties in Valencia, Venezuela. I was roaming the streets of a small town, carrying my then-two-year-old son, when a skinny older man with wild hair approached me on the street. I wouldn't have known what he said except that a nearby stranger could translate from Spanish to English. He laid his hand on my arm and excitedly gestured toward my heart. I was startled and tried to pull away, but my new-found interpreter told me to wait; the *brujo,* or shaman, had a message for me.

"You have the gift of color," the ancient man stated. "You must heal with it."

After returning home to Minnesota, I signed up for a class on healing. It was the first class ever held in the area on energetic healing. Huddled in the downstairs of a bed-and-breakfast with eight other "weird" people, I was instructed in chakraology, the energetic anatomy of chakras and auric fields. Finally, someone labeled what I'd been seeing my entire life. Imagine being able to see trees—and no one else sees them or even tells you that they can perceive them. And then one day, someone tells you that he can see trees *and* give you a name for them!

This class opened a parallel path to my spiritual journey. Before then, I'd lightly explored the invisible world for personal reasons and gain, not paying much attention to the scholarly or scientific aspects of the energetic. I now fell in love with the study of energy. I began to research and take more classes. I took advantage of every opportunity available to investigate shamanism, chakras, auric fields, and the spiritual history and science behind them.

I gulped travel like a parched desert dweller. I interviewed plant healers in Belize and Mexico, Peru and other South American countries, seeking to better understand the blessings of nature. I tracked down a native medicine shaman in the Bribri Reservation in Costa Rica to discover ways to heal contemporary concerns such as drug abuse. I spent two weeks journeying across the British Isles, stopping at three to four sacred sites a day, in order to understand the living spirit of this earth. I followed the Sahara to her edge, asking about snake medicine. I attended sweat lodges amongst the Lakota and sought the secrets to divination in the isles of Greece.

I also read—incessantly. Books about quantum physics, magazines like *Scientific American*, esoteric sacred texts and in-vogue books on healing and shamanism. I attended a Christian seminary to understand Christ and imbibed sacred medicine in Peru to learn about the greater universe. No matter the journey, internal or external, the lessons and learning always came down to an increased awareness of my Sight: my ability to see the colors, forms, energies, and shapes that act in concert with the subtle energy anatomy—the energy channels, bodies, and fields that underlie physical reality.

My course of study wasn't laboratory based. You could say I learned most of what I know in the field. My tools didn't include microscopes or telescopes. My main "sight scope" was my own internal vision, the psychic ability called clairvoyance, or "clear seeing." My medical analysis didn't involve probing the liver or intestines; instead, I investigated what others couldn't see—but millions of people over the centuries have nonetheless known, talked, and written about. Yes, I read about others' investigations into the greater mysteries, but ultimately, I used my own common sense and clairvoyance as a measuring stick.

My emerging expertise led to worldwide fame as a chakra expert. My first book, *New Chakra Healing*, published by Llewellyn over a decade ago, is now published in over a dozen languages and has been added to and reissued as *The Complete Book of Chakra Healing*. It is one of the few chakra texts that is constantly referenced and referred to by healers and energy workers everywhere. In this book, I not only catalog and reference twelve basic chakras, but twenty spiritual points as well. (If you're going to go for broke, you might as well go all the way.) I continued to share my healing expertise, which constantly draws from my clairvoyant gift, in several other books, including my most recently released reference manual, *The Subtle Body: An Encyclopedia of Your Energetic Anatomy*, the world's first and certainly most comprehensive rendering of the three main energetic systems as discussed spiritually and researched scientifically over the last five thousand years.

I'm proud of all my books, but I'm probably most pleased with the actual daily work I perform every day for individuals and organizations around the world—for real people, just like you and me. I have worked with over thirty thousand clients as a clairvoyant consultant, or an energy healer and counselor who can see pictures in her head. These images, along with corresponding words, insights, and sensations, have helped me help others help themselves. The sum total of every question answered—some of which are included in this book—is that I've figured out that we really are much more than we seem. We really are spiritual beings having a human experience.

No matter how seemingly mundane (or huge) our concern or question—whether it be about relationship, work, or health—it all reduces to the seeking of truth and a reason to embrace our divinity in and through our humanness. It all comes down to hope—the hope realized through expressions of love and joy, no matter outward appearances or inner feelings.

Here's my reasoning: if we are spiritual beings first and foremost, then all of life is basically about the manifestation of our divinity. We didn't set aside our heavenly nature when we journeyed from paradise to conduct an earthly life; we brought it with us. We don't lose the advantage of spiritual giftedness or celestial interconnection just because much of our day is taken up with the tyranny of details: the washing of dishes, the walking to work, the filling out of tax forms, the sneezing from a cold. No, we become more spiritual with every breath—with every embrace of the worldly—as long as we're devoted to the expression of love. No matter how small a smile, it's still a smile. No matter how deeply we've hidden our hearts, we still have them. No matter how many questions life has yet to answer, we're still asking them; we're still stretching for and developing into our divine nature.

If there's any goal I have for this book and for you upon reading it, it is that you will cull out the hope. You will carve and sculpt and call forth the various reasons for hoping that your life will *explode* into the brilliance that you are.

It's okay to have fears. It's okay to look back and not like some of your life—maybe even parts of your current life. In reading the questions I'm most commonly asked and my corresponding answers, I hope you realize that challenges are no reason to stop searching, living, and learning. We each have special gifts, and yours is critical to you, humankind, Earth, and the Divine. Maybe you also see pictures. Maybe you are guided through sense, knowing, words, music, touch, or sensations. Maybe your dreams have come true; maybe they have yet to come true. No matter what, there's no better time than now to embrace your gifts at every level, for indeed, the world needs all that you are and all that you can do.

**WE ARE SUCH** stuff
As dreams are made on,
And our little life
Is rounded with a sleep.

—William Shakespeare,
*The Tempest*

# Part I

# Telling Stories
## *One Picture at a Time*

Can you create a better life, one picture at a time?

Think about your past. You might view it as a unique medley of images, sensations, and flashes of understanding. Maybe it unfolds as a sort of movie in your mind. Maybe it's picturesque or placid or wildly formed or plain. Whatever it is, it can be imaged visually, can't it?

Consider your present situation. Your awareness of your present life can probably be expressed in feelings as well as images, and maybe words, tones, or songs, as well. There are many ways we understand our current lives, but the only way for us to move from the "now" into a future we might like better is to design this future, one picture at a time.

Guess your future. Your dreams and hopes appear in motion-picture imagery, don't they? The details might be hazy, the framework of events vague, but we think and shape our destiny and future with pictures colored by our personality.

If I were to look at your future, I would describe a sea of bright and infinite possibilities. I can't guarantee that all this neat stuff will happen, though; our lives are sculpted by what we do every second. "Now" is a product of where we have been. To become something different, we have to *do* something different. We have to become what we could become before we even get there.

I am an expert at pictures that form energetically when a client consults me. I see these images in my mind's eye for myself and for other people. I wish I could show them to you, as if my mind had a screen like a digital camera, because I think you'd really enjoy seeing for yourself the way that I would see you. Did you know that you are an amazing rainbow of various hues? Your problems—and the solutions for them—can be portrayed in multicolored images. You are a photographic marvel.

These visions are created by energy. Each of us has an energy system, which I describe later in this book. I am able to read your energy system as well as the energy systems of organizations, countries, and even planets, and I see this energy as pictures, colors, and symbols. Primarily, I visualize the chakras and auric fields, two of the energy systems that occupy your energetic anatomy—the structures that underlie the physical you. By peering through your skin, beyond your organs, and under your mind, I'm able to perceive the beliefs, feelings, memories, events, dreams, desires, and spirit that make you unique. If I can help you find the subtle reason for a problem, we can more easily shift physical reality, leaving you better able to design and dwell within the life you've always dreamed about.

In Part I, the section you are now reading, I discuss the importance of pictures, based on my expertise at psychic visioning. This first section narrates my own life stories. What does it mean to see pictures since before birth? What is it like to be a natural intuitive? How does this affect my view of the Divine? How did I come to accept my psychic gifts? What is it like to live a real life as a consulting psychic?

I also introduce the concept of the three spheres, which I discuss in more detail in Part II. Life can be reduced to—and celebrated through—three areas of activity: relationship or love, work or destiny, and health or balance. The Divine works (and laughs) through each of these three areas, helping us uncover the spirit that we are. As we explore our true self through these arenas, we become a vessel for creating more heaven on earth. We open more and more of our divine nature through our human "beings" and "doings."

Each of us has unique gifts; some of us accept them, and some of us reject them. Each story is distinct. My hope is that my own tale encourages you to expand beyond the boundaries you have currently established for yourself, so that you, too, can see that you have been equipped with everything you need for success.

Part of my life story is my true work—I spend my days listening to peoples' questions and asking the Divine to provide images in response. I see pictures that are customized to the person before me, but many insights bear a great deal of similarity. We humans are more alike than we are dissimilar. In Part II, I share the most common client questions I have heard, as well as responses. I think you will discover some interesting and thrilling inspirations about life in these question-and-answer chapters.

In the end, I think it comes down to a quote from Shakespeare at the start of this section. We dream our lives in pictures, as visions, images, and revelations. We can dream big or small. We can dream fearfully or joyfully. Whatever it is you dream will become your reality—one image at a time.

# Life Questions:
## *Winning the Lottery and Other Important Issues*

*Will I ever win the lottery?*

This is one of the most popular questions I am asked in my job. Other questions I hear on an almost daily basis include:

- *Do I have a soul mate?*
- *What is my spiritual mission?*
- *What will heal me?*
- *What does my future hold?*
- *Can I talk with a deceased loved one?*
- *Will I ever experience true love?*
- *Why am I here?*
- *How can I become more financially secure?*

What are my responses to these questions? The answers are different for every person that consults me, although I have been able to perceive common themes over time. Can I help everyone who asks these or other pressing life questions? Many of my clients shower me with accolades, although I have yet to provide numbers for winning the lottery. My real job is not to stop with the presented question; my job is to examine the pieces of the puzzle that form the basis of the question. Only then can we look at action steps that will shape a solution.

Is there an overdue bill? A family crisis? A hated job? If there is one overdue bill, there are more—and probably an underlying financial issue. If there is a family crisis, we must determine what constitutes "family" and who has the capacity to help or hinder. A detested job provides the opportunity to ask life's most vital questions: *What do I think I deserve? What do I think I am really worth? Why am I on this planet at this time—and how do I go about doing my true work?* I usually bring more questions to the surface (and some answers), so people can become who they are really supposed to be. Moreover, my job is to help people evaluate whether they can become more than they already are.

In other words, I provide hope.

## The Job of Seeing Hope

We all need hope. Life is challenging. How many times am I on the way to school with my youngest son, thinking I have things handled—the pets are fed, my eldest son has received his current college monies, and my younger son's backpack is stuffed with lunch, homework, and the ever-vital iPod paraphernalia—when the unexpected happens: younger son slams his hand in the car door exiting to run into school. How will I reschedule my workday, due to start in twenty minutes?

We have all had experiences like this; these are moments when we need real solutions, practical insights, and a little luck. And there are days—if not years—that we need more. There are times that require hope, which is not exactly dispensed by the local pharmacy. There are times we need to be reminded that yes, we're actually spiritual beings in a human experience, and that all this experience *really does* add up to joy.

I not only provide hope, I actually see it—in black and white and color. To me, hope is packaged in pictures.

My job is not generally recognized as a legitimate career path. It is not listed in the Internal Revenue Service's catalog of standard professions, nor did I take college classes to qualify for it, and yet, in a way, my entire life has been training for what I do.

## Clairvoyance

The word *clairvoyance* means "clear seeing." The trade is as old as humankind, as are other terms for this gift—psychic, soothsayer, mystic, seer, shaman. Stereotypically, you might picture a clairvoyant as a gypsy with a crystal ball and tarot cards; her job is to reveal your future.

If that is your expectation of me, you will be disappointed. I am a normal person—a mom, a friend, a daughter. You would not pick me out at Target, and probably not at my local coffee shop, either. I do not look much like the gypsy stereotype.

If you were to have a session with me, I would see pictures for you—just for you. Lots of pictures. Some pictures would represent your personality; other pictures might show your hidden desires, deep needs, spiritual purpose, and petty jealousies. Some images might reveal painful memories, bad habits, or a bizarre fantasy. Still other imagery might depict a future love or a possible life path. These images might appear on my mind-screen in reaction to your questions, or some might come unbidden.

I do not choose what pictures I am going to see, but I need to be able to interpret them. You might ask questions; I might ask questions. Ultimately, however, a strange mix of your unconscious, your energy system, my innate ability, and the Divine determines the pictures appearing in my mind's eye and sometimes through my physical eyes too. What shows up is sometimes entertaining, frequently poignant, and often heartrending—but always interesting.

Everyone wants pictures that help reveal more about who they are as a person. That is why I've worked with over thirty thousand clients and reach even more people with my workshops and books. It is my job to see, say, learn, and advise. It is my job to be a clairvoyant.

## What's in a Picture?

At various times in our lives, we all need insight from a source outside ourselves. When facing legal issues, we turn to a lawyer; for emotional dilemmas, a therapist; for medical questions, a doctor. We turn to specialists to help us with specific problems. We turn to clairvoyants when we require an intuitive specialist who can look beneath appearances to see what is really going on.

Clairvoyance is not only used to convey impressions; it can deliver advice, predictions, and healing. The Delphic oracles of ancient Greece are among the most well-known clairvoyants in history. The Delphic oracle was usually an older woman from the local area with a special gift, sometimes called "the Sight." Entering a trance state, she would offer prophecy, usually in riddle form. In turn, the temple priests interpreted this prediction. The Delphic oracles were consulted for nearly everything—government matters, household concerns, and affairs of the heart.

Alexander the Great, the conqueror of the known world circa 350 BCE, attributed much of his own military success to the Oracle of Amon at the Siwa Oasis in Egypt. It is not known what the oracle told Alexander, but many researchers speculate that the oracle not only predicted his conquest but also whispered tactical advice. Presumably in gratitude, Alexander thereafter expressed a wish to be buried at the Siwa Oasis.

Joseph, son of Jacob (from the story in the Torah, Koran, and Old Testament), was a Hebrew boy whose brothers sold him into slavery. Through a series of misadventures, he was eventually thrown into prison in Egypt. This seemingly dismal event was actually an opportunity for Joseph's gifts to be noticed. The word spread from prison that Joseph was adept at interpreting dreams. In time, the pharaoh heard of Joseph's ability and called Joseph before him to ask for an interpretation of a disturbing dream. Joseph foresaw years of plenty and then years of famine. He also saw a way to plan for the lean years. The pharaoh appointed him vizier, granting Joseph the power needed to enact these strategies. Thanks to Joseph, Egypt did not suffer during the famine.

Shamans, priest-healers of indigenous communities, have long used clairvoyant visions to diagnose illnesses and deliver healing. They are able to stretch beyond the bounds of the physical plane to perceive the invisible, speak with the inaudible, and move energy that is "there" to "here" for curing their patients. I have been fortunate enough to study with clairvoyants and healers all over the world, in places including Japan, Costa Rica, Belize, Mexico, Hawaii, Russia, Wales, England, Greece, and Morocco. I have learned that this gift transcends ethnic, religious, and language boundaries; the gift itself is transcendent.

What is in a picture? Everything, including the means to reexamine the past, shift the present, and create the future. It is only one of many possible psychic gifts. There are verbal gifts such as mediumship, channeling, and telepathy; spiritual kinesthetic, or sensing, gifts, which evolve through means including prayer and meditation; and physical kinesthetic gifts, which comprise psychometry and sensing others' feelings.

You have at least one—if not many—of these gifts. They are structured into your energy system, namely the chakras or energy centers just inside and outside of your body, via your spirit. Your spirit is that special and unique part of you that knows itself as loved and connected to the Divine, no matter what the external circumstances are. These "unusual" gifts are spiritual gifts, necessary to the fulfillment of your special earthly purpose. To know your gifts is to know yourself; to know yourself is to unfold— and use—your gifts. We are here to share our gifts with each other and, by doing so, share joy with the Divine.

## What Happens in a Session

Clairvoyance, as well as the other spiritual gifts, is used for infinite reasons. Often, my clients come in during times of transition in their own lives, with a list of questions. *Should I take this job? Is my mother okay? Should I get married? Why am I sick?*

In response to a question, I usually see an image that gets us started. I see visions in my head, although sometimes the images appear through my physical eyes. Unlike many people in my profession, I actually keep my eyes open when I'm working. I think that eye contact with my client is important; I understand that it can be uncomfortable to spend an hour staring at someone who has her eyes closed while you're talking about deep, sensitive matters.

These internal pictures often provide insight, healing, or perspective. They might serve as a warning, a foreshadowing, or a dose of wisdom. They can reference the past, describe a situation in the present, or predict a future event. Sometimes the energy of the picture makes the client feel agitated because it stirs up issues. On occasion, the pictures deliver a healing, and an illness or problem completely disappears.

My favorite activity is to see colors. My internal world has a palette of colors rich with nuances and meaning. Colors describe the world; to me, people are unique composites of colors that continually evolve and shift.

I can only interpret the message of a color within the context of the picture. For instance, I can read someone's basic personality by the location of colors "on" their body. Imagine a bold cherry red splashed across someone's hip area. The placement of the bright red tells me that my client is a passionate, adventuresome person who could never work for someone else. A muddy red in the same area informs me about a stuck issue, probably an addiction. No red at all? That person is exhausted and probably physically ill. A picture of a red cat, however, might have any number of meanings. Maybe my client owns a red cat or should adopt a red cat. Most likely, however, a strange image is metaphorical, and I will ask the Divine for further interpretation. Perhaps the person is like a red cat, maybe he or she was a red cat in a past life, or perhaps he or she just bought a red Jaguar vehicle.

These colors relate to those ascribed to the various chakras and auric layers in the energy system. I know what the colors represent because each symbolizes a different theme. In general, the meaning of a color will correspond to the interpretation of a chakra of the same color. The first chakra, located in the hip area, is red. This chakra rep–

resents power, passion, activity, security, and primal feelings. If I see red somewhere on someone's body, I know that I'm dealing with similar types of descriptors.

One of my life pursuits has involved cataloguing the various energetic systems in and around the body, including energy channels such as the meridians and nadis, rivers that transport life energy; energy bodies, including the chakras, which translate psychic to physical energy and vice versa; and energy fields such as the auric field, which serve as boundaries and filters. Energy bodies such as the chakras are vibrational in nature. Each of the many chakras runs on its own vibratory band, the frequency describable as tone, function, and color. My books, including *The Complete Book of Chakra Healing* and *The Subtle Body: An Encyclopedia of Your Energetic Anatomy*, are devoted to figuring out ways to apply this frequency-based knowledge to the creation of a joyful life.

Symbols and shapes also provide clues to what is going on in a client's life, as does the nature of the image. Colors and shapes tell me a lot. For example, depression shows up as a black box. I can determine the cause of the depression by analyzing its location in someone's body. If the black box is situated in the throat, I know that the issues involved will relate to the fifth chakra, the chakra located in the throat. I now surmise that my client grew up with verbal abuse and has communication challenges, one of the main functions of the fifth chakra. If the black box is in the abdomen, I know that he or she has a lot of sadness and repressed anger, and has difficulties with self-expression and revealing his or her originality. This area is managed by the second chakra, home of feelings and creativity. If that black box is in the heart, very likely my client is experiencing a challenging relationship. Guess what the fourth chakra, located in the heart, represents? Yes, love and relationships.

Many images are stubborn. Sometimes I see only a single picture, which does not disappear until I describe it. I had this happen early in my career, and I almost quit on the spot during a particular session. I did not see how the only image that appeared—popcorn—was going to answer any questions for my client.

My client had asked about an affair she was having, and honestly, all I could see was an image of popcorn. I tried to bat the picture out of my mind, but it wouldn't budge. Finally, an angel came into focus, but all she did was hold a picture of a bag of popcorn in the center of my mind-screen, as if to say, "Do what you want; this picture isn't going anywhere." I finally mentioned the image to my client. She burst into tears!

"I have a popcorn addiction," she confessed, and then she described her lifelong battle with popcorn. She ate it for breakfast and lunch. She'd go to a movie in the middle of the day just to eat a large-sized popcorn bucket, and then she'd leave the movie when the container was empty. She even hid popcorn under the front seat of her car.

During our session, we uncovered the deeper trauma that led to this addiction: my client's father had deserted the family when she was only three years old.

"The only memory I have of my father is going to a movie and eating popcorn with him," my client confessed.

Now I understood the reason that she was addicted to popcorn. The deeper craving was for a father's love. At this point, my client and I were able to discuss the reasons she was involved in an affair and the real issue she was facing, the lack of intimacy in her marriage. She had married a man just like her father. While her father had been physically missing, her husband was emotionally absent. Even if I didn't, the Divine knew the story would unfold with the picture of popcorn.

Usually one image opens to another and then to another, providing me an ongoing filmstrip. I have watched events as joyful as a happy holiday party, as tragic as the death of a child, and as shocking as years spent in a concentration camp. I have viewed accidents I have wanted to prevent and was unable to, as well as illnesses that were caught in time to prevent death. I cannot control the pictures or messages that I receive. I can only offer what I am seeing, sensing, feeling, and hearing, and leave the rest to my client—and to the Divine.

## Don't Shoot the Messenger

Once in a while, a client doesn't like what I've said. Sometimes I'm wrong. I might misinterpret a vision or misunderstand the meaning of an intuitive insight. I might also explain it wrong. That happens; I'm human. Sometimes a client misconstrues what I say. This happens most frequently if the issue is sensitive. For instance, one woman heard me saying that she shouldn't be having an affair (that she was having), when what I really said was that we might want to take a look at why she was having one. Her guilt twisted the message, and she became quite irate.

Yet another time, an elderly man came in with his daughter. They wanted me to connect with her deceased mother, his wife. I cautioned them. All intuitives have specialties; connecting to the other side isn't my favorite activity. Nonetheless, I provided as much input as I could.

I clearly heard the deceased mother ask her daughter for forgiveness. Apparently, the mother had struck the daughter several times. The father sprang up and began to yell at me, insisting that I was lying. His daughter began crying and stated that the information was true. The father continued to yell, and I asked him to control himself or leave. I pointed out that just because I was serving as a vessel for information didn't mean that I wasn't a person. Just as I grant clients respect, I ask for it in return.

Most of the time, people are very kind and respectful, even if they don't believe in clairvoyance or any other form of intuition. They are also forgiving of my mistakes, especially as I inform them at the beginning of a session that intuition—especially in regard to future prediction—can only be about 80 percent accurate. This is due to human error and also the fact that there are simply some things that aren't supposed to be known. Who or what makes this decision? Perhaps the Divine or the divine aspect of the client decides that certain aspects of life need to be lived, not pre-digested. Once in a while, I think my own inner self, or spirit, overrides the client's needs and hides information from me. I felt like this happened during a session with one particular gentleman who came in with a gun under his suit. I knew that he was a Mafia godfather. Although I provided him messages encouraging self-forgiveness and a change of heart, I never received the brutal images that would have explained his former activities; probably neither of us would have been served. In general, the ethics of being a reader are the same as any other service profession. I act as respectful and polite as possible, and in turn require a similar attitude.

## The Spirituality of Tragedy

Through my work, I have touched many human tragedies. One of my most painful client-session memories involves a woman who lost her entire family—her husband, mother, and two children—to a drunk-driving accident.

A teenage boy had been drinking all night. He lost control of his car at 7 AM, just when the family had pulled away from their home to drive to Florida for a vacation. The boy's car careened into my client's. She turned her neck to warn her children and mother, who were sitting in the back seat. This position caused her to be missed when several steel beams, previously attached to the boy's car, came through the car. One beam impaled her husband and other beams were heaved through the back seat, killing everyone.

My client wanted to know why this had happened.

The Divine took me through the senses and feelings experienced by each member of the family just before death. I am not a medium, and I do not channel the dead. Nonetheless, the Divine used me to provide this poor woman with the grace of knowing that each member of her family had left his or her body before feeling pain. I was even able to hear messages from each one, providing my client with details about their lives after death and their wishes for her. During the session, the only image I could see was of a bright white light, the light of the Divine.

There was no explanation for the tragedy. The Divine does not sit in heaven plotting each move in our three-dimensional world. But there was compassion for this woman's loss—and an enduring love.

While one aspect of the human experience is painful, others can be just plain ridiculous. An example is Susan, who had never been married. She asked about a potential soul mate, and the only picture I could see was of a scarecrow in khaki pants and a denim shirt. Neither of us could make sense of the picture, so we dismissed it.

Three years later, Susan called, inviting me to her wedding. "Guess what hangs in my closet?" she asked. "My fiancé leaves khaki pants and a denim shirt at my house to use when he spends the night." She continued, "Our first date was to watch *The Wizard of Oz*, at which time he told me that his favorite character was the scarecrow!"

Susan believed that the psychic image received years earlier in our session had helped her to recognize her future mate.

While I do not discount the traumas and intense pain of life experiences, I do recognize that the walk of human life is one of extremes—of death, life, separations, connections, mastery, and mistakes.

Many people ask me if my life is perfect because I have the ability to "see." Those close to me sometimes ask why I am not more perfect, given that I can "see." My life is characterized by mistakes and successes, like everyone else's. I have realized, however, that every predicament has been accompanied by the gift of divine grace. Every error, while not erasable, can be transformed. All visions lead to enlightenment, even those that show us what mistakes we have made that day.

It was not easy, growing up clairvoyant. Nor is it easy to be a clairvoyant, making a living with my clairvoyance. I am not spared any grief, but I do know that there can be a gift within the grief.

And it all started with a series of tea parties...

CHILDREN OFTEN HAVE imaginary playmates.
I suspect that half of them are really
their guardian angels.

—Eileen Elias Freeman,
*The Angels' Little Instruction Book*

# Enlightenment in a Teacup

The angels fold their wings carefully over the edge of the table, making sure they don't knock the china off my child-size table. They nod with great, glowing smiles as I serve the make-believe tea in miniature cups. A friend has accompanied them; he doesn't have wings, but I like him.

They are very polite, my angels and their friend, as they initiate well-mannered small talk, customized to me, their four-year-old audience.

Has Suzy's hair grown back? (Suzy is my bald doll. Besides lacking hair, she is missing an arm. My guests politely refrain from that topic, as it is emotionally charged.) How about Barbie? Does she have some new dresses? Has *her* hair grown back? (I played hairdresser to all my companion dolls one day—a good fifteen of them were shorn in a single hour.) How had my mother reacted to my most recent experiment, the manufacturing of perfume from "toilet water"? (It is a completely understandable mistake, soothes angel Gabriel. After all, the perfume was labeled "eau de toilette." Why not create new aromas by mixing *real* toilet water with the eau de toilette?)

To hear the gurus tell it, enlightenment must begin with a miraculous feat, divine inspiration, or the realization of perfection. My path to enlightenment started with these tea parties.

I do not remember the first time my best friends, the angels, began to attend my tea parties, but I know that they changed my life. Before them, I was lonely. My family had moved, and there weren't many children my age to play with. There were my younger sisters, but they were too young to relate to me. I felt strange and unusual and was scared that no one could or would ever understand me. Along came the angels, who met me right exactly where I was: dolls, dress-up clothes, and tea parties. I suppose if I had been more the cowboy type, then the angels would have ridden ponies, too. The angels showed an odd little girl that she was lovable and managed to work in a few stealthy lesson plans too.

One evening, Gabriel (who had wings) handed me a large volume entitled *The Book of Knowledge*. I remember the *aha!* feeling that accompanied my reading of it. Suddenly I understood why the world had come into being, why people existed, even why I had come to Earth. Unfortunately, I cannot remember a word of this book today.

Another time, Gabriel accompanied me to the park, where he showed me the wonders of nature. Not only did we watch caterpillars crawl and robins fly, but he showed me the world *within* the world—that of fairies and other small creatures visible only to the knowing eye.

The female angel, Lucy, only revealed herself when I was sad. She would comfort me, telling me that some day, life would be happier. The third tea party attendee wasn't really an angel. He was a thin man with dark hair and a beard, robed like the men in the Sunday school picture books. He was kind, although he did not talk much. I believe he was Jesus.

The angels were only part of my little universe. I heard ghosts in the house, saw colors around people, listened to the fairies, and heard poetry in the wind. I didn't know that I was unusual—not until my parents began to scoff at what I said. Later, they warned me about the devil and demons.

It took me a while to learn that I was not supposed to share what was real to me with anyone. Eventually, I stopped sharing myself altogether. I believe that most of us do this.

If you were to look inside yourself, would you find a little girl or boy who, like me, could see the invisible, talk to the angels, feel another's feelings, tend to animals, or know what the Divine is thinking? Through my work, I have discovered that most of our "real selves" actually live in the past, and that we cannot be who we really are until we return to find him or her.

## The Reality Before Reality

When a client is really caught up in issues—when life is unhappy and there is no movement whatsoever—I return him or her to the past.

When working, I calm my client, help him or her breathe deeply, and encourage a looser grip on current reality. We now drift backward, my client transformed into a leaf, a feather, or a gust of air. We invite the Divine to guide us back into the situation that created the original problem—the beginning of the problem—for there, we will make the changes that will reverberate into the present and beyond.

My own life concerns started back in the womb, in fact. I was traumatized in such a way that I remained locked in a state of terror until I worked through the pain as an adult. The same situation that created these future problems for me, however, also activated my clairvoyance. The wound created the light that has guided me through my life.

My first memory is of being nestled inside my mother, perhaps a few months past conception, listening to the *lub-dub* poetry of her heart and the *shush-shush* of the blood cycling through her body. I was aware of a glow of energy around my skin, which I would now call God, and the softness of the salty water outside of that. I now recall this time period every time I hold a pearl. I think of life as having a sound—that of the rubbing of saltwater against a particle of sand, which, when troubled enough, forms a pearl. The price of beauty, of our true self, is a similarly painful process.

Life was sound and sensation. There wasn't yet any light. At some point, however, I became aware of the sounds from outside of the womb, my haven, and these sounds weren't good.

My parents were fighting. I could hear their words and sense the anger and hatred they held for each other. I felt cushioned from these intense emotions until, suddenly, it was as if my eyes, previously blind, were opened wide.

Their words penetrated the womb like spears. These words had colors and shapes, and these colors and shapes were frightening and scary. Each hurt me in a different way and formed fears inside of me. Over time, these fears solidified into negative, self-destructive patterns, such as food disorders, panic attacks, feelings of unworthiness in relationships, and codependency.

Years of therapy and self-growth work helped me realize these patterns, but only a return to their point of origin helped me actually heal from inside and draw different situations into my life.

My parents' brutal, saddening treatment of each other injured me, but it also awakened the key to my spiritual mission: my clairvoyance. Whatever the purpose, I am grateful that my gift was activated; I would rather "see" what I am dealing with than just sense or hear it. Similarly, I'm convinced that each of us would rather see the monster under the bed than simply to hear it making noises.

If we look into the shadows, we will eventually see light. Once we behold what frightens us, we can deal with it; we can negotiate, embrace, or transform it. We all have special gifts that can help us do this—the gifts that we may have suppressed since childhood.

## Through the Eyes of a Child

We all have unique abilities, but we often surrender them to childhood as "make-believe." Western society classifies capabilities by appearance and effect, rather than by their internal truth and meaning. As an adult, how often do you introduce or explain yourself with statements like "I am gifted at knowing" or "I see pictures that help others see themselves the way that God sees them"? Usually, we introduce ourselves by describing what we do to make money: *I am a chef, I am a mechanical engineer, I am a network administrator, I am a doctor.*

We confine our children to the same boxes, forcing them to describe themselves with nonmagical definitions—no drawing outside the lines! *I am a kindergartner, a seventh grader, a philosophy undergraduate. I am good at art, science, or languages. I excel at sports.*

Many Eastern spiritualities and most indigenous communities understand that the surface world is only that—the surface. What counts is what is underneath. What is real is the spirit of a person, which most children understand.

One young client, Maggie, voiced the truth eloquently when her mother brought her to see me.

Maggie's head was bandaged. She had a terminal brain tumor and although she'd had three surgeries, the tumor kept coming back. She knew she wasn't going to live. This is what she had to say to her mother, who was crying and asking for a miracle: "Mommy, it's okay. Even when my body is gone, I'm not."

Maggie understood that a person isn't who they are because of what is on his or her outsides. It is the insides that count—and our ability to express them externally.

## Seeing Colors

A favorite activity of mine as a child was watching the colors around people. Just before her temper exploded, my mother's energy would turn red—all of her, not only her face. I learned never to ask for anything unless a soft pink glow surrounded her.

My father had only to lift an alcoholic beverage and his body would be enveloped in a cloud of muddy brown. He drank every night, so he was brown quite often. He would, however, arrive home from work with a vivid green emanating from his heart. I could tell he was happy, and I would rush to hug him. Unfortunately, he and my mother would soon be arguing, and a spaghetti-noodle mass of gray cords would spring up between them. My mother's energy would dim or flame into a brilliant red and my father's would become black, not just brown.

I am not sure what my own colors did in reaction, but I could watch the shifts in my sisters' energy. My middle sister was usually a vivid yellow, with beautiful rainbow colors that sparkled from various areas in her body. My adult esoteric studies suggest that yellow means intelligence, and that she is: a brilliant woman with a PhD and a string of achievements behind her. At dinnertime, however, with the interaction between my parents being cruel, the beautiful yellow color would turn off, and the light would dim. The sparkly colors oozed into a low gray light, and I knew that she was hiding herself.

My youngest sister was a dazzling kaleidoscope of soft, pastel colors, with a vivid peacock blue overwhelming them all. Blue signifies communication; she is a corporate vice president and also has a gifted operatic voice. When my parents would fight, however, the colors would zip into a black line that ran up and down her body. She literally zipped herself up to stay safe.

Watching the colors was an endless source of fascination for me. People weren't the only beings I watched. All animals and plant life, and even many physical objects, emanate colors. I knew that anything with a color was alive and conscious, that only the inanimate was colorless. My parent's car, which my dad called Murgatroid, was alive. When he talked to her, the dashboard would glow with this smiley white energy when he said she was doing a good job.

I made it a practice to talk to anything that had color. I recall standing in the middle of a field, attracted to a plant that was beaming a bright, sunny energy. It had a small, unopened bud, and I was struck by an idea. I asked the plant to please open the flower. The bud burst open, and a brilliant purple and white blossom popped out.

Being four years old, I picked the flower and ran to my dad.

"Daddy, the plant made a flower when I asked it to!" I laughed. He looked at me and frowned. "Cyndi, don't talk nonsense. Plants don't listen or talk."

Later discussions with my father assured me that he, in fact, believed me, but that he was scared for me. We were a Lutheran family. We didn't believe in nonsense like energy, ghosts, and fairies—well, actually, we did, but they were considered the marks of Satan. Anything non-biblically supernatural was considered to be on the devil's side.

By attitudes like these, how many children are forced to pretend that they don't see and hear what they really do see and hear? Those invisible playmates? I believe that most of them are real. We all have spiritual guides, usually two of them, that remain with us from birth through death. Some cultures also call upon animal and plant spirits as well as other elemental beings such as the spirits of living rocks and hallowed places, sacred mountains and deceased ancestors. A community of caring beings surrounds us. Usually, however, only children see them—or the child still within us.

Later in life, I learned to correlate the colors I could see with chakras and energy systems. Different cultures have different ways to explain the energetic world, but the energy beneath what we see with our physical eyes provides so many more clues about what is really happening.

## What Children See

In my practice, I find that many children are troubled and sometimes injured by their parents' ignorance of the spiritual world. One little girl, Sonia, kept insisting that a "pretty angel" visited her bedside at night to tell stories. Her parents thought this flight of imagination was harmless enough, until Sonia became agitated by one of the stories, which predicted an airplane accident for her father. Apparently, the "imagined" being even gave a date, six months from the warning.

Sonia's parents scoffed at the "ghost story," becoming angrier as Sonia became more insistent. They grew concerned, however, when Sonia began to cry constantly and refuse to sleep at night. Her appetite failed, and she told them that the pretty angel would not come until the father listened to her. Nothing stopped Sonia's "obsession"—not a lecture from the doctor, not a visit to the psychologist, not even the threat of no Christmas presents. At wit's end, Sonia's parents brought her to see me.

Sonia huddled under one of my blankets, thin and sullen, while her mother talked. Sonia refused to look at me, until her mother, having told the story, told me that Sonia's father did, in fact, have a prescheduled trip to Europe for the dates in the warning.

I reflected on Sonia's tale. After thinking about the best way to handle the situation, I decided to ask a simple question.

"What if the warning is true?" I asked.

Sonia's mother looked at me, astonished.

I phrased the question another way. "What if there really is an angel, and she really is giving you a warning?"

I believed Sonia. My inner images suggested that there really might be an upcoming accident. Not all predictions come to pass, but many have at least a grain of truth, and this one seemed to have that. I asked Sonia's mother if there was any harm in accepting Sonia's vision. Would it really cost so much, financially or emotionally, to reschedule the trip for a later date? Sonia's mother huffed, but her daughter looked a little lighter and brighter.

I received a call a few weeks later. For some reason, Sonia's parents had followed my advice and pushed her father's trip out another month. The plane he would have been on did, in fact, crash. Everyone aboard died.

*

I find that many children are able to see, hear, or sense the extraordinary. Quite simply, they see the reality underneath reality. Our culture tends to think it is only girls that dabble in the intuitive, and therefore discounts their abilities. Boys also have gifts, as shown by this story about a boy named Nasser.

Nasser was a twelve-year-old East Indian boy who came to see me with his mother. He would only wear a certain pair of pants, held up with a piece of rope. He was so skinny that I could see his ribs. His mother informed me that he would only eat yogurt and nuts, as he did not want to be responsible for the killing of anything that was alive. With his long hair—he wouldn't allow it to be cut—Nasser looked like a tiny version of an old-fashioned guru.

I asked what was going on, and his mother said that Nasser spent hours gazing into space. Could I break through? Could I form a lifeline to this young man?

For his part, Nasser simply sat before me, saying nothing. I prayed for guidance. Immediately, I envisioned a Bionicle, an action figure that my younger son collects. We have Bionicle parts all over the house.

"You like Bionicles!" I guessed, and Nasser's eyes lit up. I ran upstairs and retrieved a few, and he started to play with them. I had another picture leap in my head, that of a Bionicle coming alive.

I knew, then, that Nasser—like myself as a child—could perceive animate, or conscious, energy in objects.

"You can see which Bionicles are alive and which are not," I stated.

At that moment, Nasser flew into a rage and began to yell at his mother, accusing her of telling me his secret.

This young man did have a secret: he was gifted. Like many other children, he could see what others could not see. He saw images, colors, visions, filmstrips, words, realities, possibilities, metaphors, and stories of what had been, what is, and what could be. He was carrying on a long tradition, one that is full of potential but also danger.

Danger of being unaccepted.

Danger of being unacknowledged.

Danger of becoming our true selves.

I'd like to say that there was a happy ending to Nasser's story, but I'm not sure there is. I helped his mother better relate to him and her other children, who were equally gifted. Last I knew, however, there wasn't a school Nasser was comfortable in—or that was comfortable with him—and so he was being home-schooled. Perhaps our world needs to create better options for the children who carry such sacred gifts.

**THE ONLY THING** we have to fear is fear itself—
nameless, unreasoning, unjustified terror, which paralyzes
needed efforts to convert retreat into advance.

—Franklin Delano Roosevelt's
first inaugural address, 4 March 1933

# What Goes *Bump* in the Middle of the Night

Honey is the name of our wild-dog golden retriever. His full name is Honey Bunny, and at age six, he is still a real handful. Recently, a friend pointed out that there are dog-training courses. My younger son, Gabe, who is Honey's best friend, replied, "We know. We've done two of them."

There are four important things in Honey's life: Gabe, whom he sleeps with every night; food—a devotion that has earned him many dinners he wasn't invited to eat; walking—enabling him to fulfill his spiritual mission of ridding the world of squirrels; and his tail.

Honey loves his tail. Since he believes himself to be a boy, he thinks the only thing wrong with the other boys in the world is that they lack a tail. This makes him their handsome superior. He preens in front of the mirror, watching it wag. He frees it of alien objects, such as burrs and weeds, before he walks in the house. And he chases it. Constantly.

It took me a while to consider that I should apply my clairvoyant ability to Honey's tail, but I finally did, tired of things crashing to the floor when he would suddenly begin to chase his tail. There actually *was* something supernatural going on. Through my psychic vision, I saw a small brown elf straddling Honey's tail. I could see that this little man thought himself a warrior; he was vehemently stabbing Honey's tail with his blade, and I could almost hear him shouting "Take that!" as he valiantly tried to vanquish what to him must be a ferocious giant.

Later, I called an intuitive friend, whom I knew had an affiliation with the fairy realm, and asked her about the little warrior. "He's a house elf," she told me.

"Hmmm," I reflected, wondering what else a house elf might do. "Can he be coached into doing the laundry?" I asked, hopefully.

She laughed. "You're thinking of the elves and the shoemaker story. No, your elf will pull pranks unless you feed him."

In a house with five animals, I could only imagine the problems if the wrong living creature indulged in elf food. Then I made the mistake of telling Gabriel about the house elf.

"Mommy, we have to feed him," he informed me with great seriousness. "What would happen if he hurt Honey because we ignored him?"

I sighed. I knew that once Gabe discovered a worry, he'd be chewing on it all night. *There goes my sleep*, I thought. So I put out a saucer of elf food that night, hoping that the elf adventure was on its way to a successful completion.

I had no such luck. Later that night, Gabriel came out of his bedroom and looked at me, obviously disconcerted.

"Mommy, can you hear the elves?"

"Yes, a little," I replied, certain I really had heard the warrior cry of the one who had attacked Honey's tail.

"Can you see them?" he asked.

"I saw one," I responded, honestly.

"Well, I can't do either," he frowned, disappointed. He became quiet, and for one hopeful moment, I thought that maybe we could have a peaceful night after all. As we sat together on his bed, I realized he was thinking.

"Mommy, how about if you put your ear next to mine and listen to the elves? Then I'll hear them through your ears." And he snuggled up next to me, putting his ear next to mine.

"I hear them!" He suddenly cried out and began to tell me what they were saying. Pretty soon, he was also telling me what they looked like, explaining them as dashes of color. That is how, thanks to Honey and his tail, we met the elves that live with us.

My world—the world of the clairvoyant, the world of a child—is full of strange and wonderful creatures, such as the house elf. There are good ones and not-so-good ones, and there are the really, really bad ones. I have seen many different types, and what I can't see can probably still see me.

Much of my work relies upon being able to see and make contact with these invisible creatures. My own life decisions have sometimes depended upon connections made with all things that go bump in the night—the energies, entities, spirits, and beings that interact with us all the time. Probably many of your life decisions have depended on these unseen creatures, whether you know it or not. As I share my own stories, you might want to reach back into your childhood—into the dreamlands you thought were make-believe—and uncover some of the memorable but physically invisible events that have shaped you. To create the future, it is important to see through the physical plane and into the energetic spiritual plane, for those are the forces that create the "matter" that matters to us.

## The Hobo Ghosts

Almost everyone asks me if I believe in ghosts. I do. I have been seeing and hearing them since I was a small girl.

My first experience with ghosts occurred when I was five years old. I awoke one evening because of a loud crash in the kitchen. Startled, I began to get out of bed, when I heard voices.

"Mac, you have to quiet it down. There are kids and a dog and such things, and You Know Who has a law against scaring the little ones."

*Mac? Who was Mac?* I wondered. My dad's name was Wally, and I certainly didn't think he'd be up, banging around the kitchen in the middle of the night.

Another voice piped in. "Aw, Harry, it's a greasy skillet, and it slips."

And the two voices proceeded to bump around the kitchen doing what sounded like an awful lot of cooking. At one point, I was certain I heard the sizzling of bacon, the chewing of crunchy toast, and at least one deep sigh of satisfaction.

I was frozen with fear and carefully stretched the covers over my head. Who were these strange men? What were they doing in our kitchen? Why hadn't my mom and dad woken up and stopped them?

Finally, the noisy intruders finished cooking and eating, and I heard a couple of belches and then a moment of silence. I thought perhaps that they were gone, but when I peeked out from under the covers, I spied shadows in the hallway, just outside my bedroom. *Oh, no! Were they coming to get me?*

I heard a door open. "Well, time to catch a train," muttered the one named Mac. Suddenly, the house was quiet.

I settled back onto my pillow. Okay, I had figured them out. They were hobos. We lived close to train tracks. Mac and Harry had obviously decided to pilfer our pantry before hopping a train.

I jumped out of bed, suddenly eager to tell my mom what had just happened. Then I thought better of it. My mom would be furious because they didn't do the dishes. I had not heard any water running, which meant that the sink would be piled with dirty pans and plates. My need for a hug overwhelmed my worry, however, and I ran into my parents' room and threw myself onto the bed.

"Mommy, Daddy, the hobos were cooking in our kitchen!"

I repeated my announcement, since my parents were a little slow coming out of sleep. Finally, my mother struggled to her feet, her hair awry, and followed me into the kitchen.

It was spick-and-span, just like when we went to bed the evening before.

My dad stood in the kitchen doorway, a look of frustration on his face. "Cyndi, you have to stop telling these stories." And with that, I was sent back to bed.

## Likable Ghosts

Most ghosts are likable. Although my hobo visitors were a bit messy—at least, in theory—they were harmless. Some ghosts are actually beneficial, as was the one I met in a swamp.

I loved spending time alone in the swamp near our house. One day, a young man walked up to me. He was dressed in tattered clothing and carried a large gray backpack. I wasn't scared; he seemed nice, if a bit sad.

He sat next with me and began fiddling with his pack, then finally began speaking, telling me that I needed to be careful in the woods because there were many dangers. "What do you mean?" I asked. I was thinking these were *my* woods; these were safe woods.

This was decades ago, before there were widespread alerts about child kidnappers or other crimes.

The man said that he had been hurt and was now helping to keep others safe. Would I like to be safe?

"Of course," I said.

He told me to stay out of the swampy woods for the next week. Then he reached into his backpack and pulled out a metal bracelet. I held it and looked up to thank him, but he had disappeared. I examined the silver bracelet and noticed that it had a name on it, as well as three letters: *MIA*.

I was in second grade, and the Vietnam War was going on. I knew very little about it, but I had seen these bracelets on my friends and knew that they were somehow related to the war. I rushed home and showed the bracelet to my father, who said that MIA meant "missing in action." "The name on this bracelet is a soldier who is missing, Cyndi," he told me. I had the sense that this particular soldier was probably dead, although at the time, I didn't link him to my swamp visitor.

My soldier's warning stuck, however. For an entire week, I avoided the swamp. Later, my mom told me that a friend of mine had been walking near the swamp one day that week and had been attacked.

I believe that the stranger who warned me was a ghost, probably the soldier that was missing in action, whose name was on that bracelet.

## Relatives Who Visit

Most ghostly visitations are from souls that we have known. Almost every day, a client reports contact with a deceased loved one. I have one client whose deceased husband, according to her, shows up as a robin outside of her window. It appears whenever she is crying, regardless of time of day, and sings a melody unlike any other robin.

Yet another client shared that her deceased mother appears in her dreams. Her mother wears her favorite housedress and usually carries a plate of cookies, the same type she most frequently baked when my client was a child. As my client-child snacks on cookies, her mother dispenses advice.

In my adult life, my own father has a penchant for showing up. And in common with my clients who have ghostly relatives visit them, there has been no personality change.

My dad loved to fix things. Every night, he would disappear into the basement or the garage to make or retool cabinets or build model airplanes. A few years ago, a friend stayed with me for a short time while searching for a place to live. My friend worked in the construction field. One day he looked at me, puzzled.

"Who's Wally?" he asked.

"That was my dad's name," I replied. "Why?"

"Well, some spirit named Wally keeps following me around your house, telling me what I need to fix. It's really annoying."

Connecting with the dead and with guides, angels, and other beings and energies is one of the keys to the clairvoyant profession. How would I have known that Ben, a new client who recently called from Maine, had a tumor, if his deceased father, a physician, hadn't shown me a picture of it? After relaying the message, the ghostly father reminisced about a fishing trip he had taken with a ten-year-old Ben, just so Ben would know it was true. If Ben had not caught the tumor when he did, his oncologist said he would have been dead within a year.

Why do angels and our deceased contacts come to us with information? They still care about us. They deliver messages from the Divine. They want to warn us about something. They want to say they are sorry for something they did when they were alive. They provide inspiration. They offer assurance. Or, perhaps, they are coming to help us on our own journey from life to death.

How are life and death linked? Where does the body store the spirit that later soars free? We don't really know how the universe works.

As stated in my favorite Bible verse from the First Epistle of Paul to the Corinthians (13, verse 11):

> WHEN I WAS a child, I spake as a child,
> I understood as a child, I thought as a child:
> but when I became a man, I put away
> childish things. For now we see through a
> glass, darkly; but then face to face: now
> I know in part; but then shall I know even
> as also I am known.

It is not for us always to understand everything that happens when it is happening.

## Unlikable Ghosts

My parents meant well, but my gifts frightened them. There are reasons to fear the unknown; sometimes what goes *bump* actually bites.

I was initiated into the truth of bad spirits when I was only a child. I saw more than colors in and around people; I could also perceive external influences—the creepy kind.

There were two spirits that periodically plagued my mother. One was tall and black, and the other was squat and gray. They looked like men, except they lacked clear features. It was as if they had been carved out of smoky clouds.

They took turns entering into and exiting from the top of my mother's head. Once they were inside her, all I could see was a thin film of energy around her head. The rest of their bodies would be inside her. Then she would act funny—*weird* funny.

When the tall spirit occupied her, my mother became angry. One moment, she would be happy and smiling, finding solutions to problems, and the next moment she would be argumentative and punishing. The tall being usually took over in the mornings; he would tell my mother what to make for breakfast. For weeks, I had to eat hard-boiled eggs for breakfast—I hated them. The rest of the family ate the type of food I liked, like Lucky Charms or sausage and toast. The fat being took over at night and usually made my mom depressed. After he slipped inside, she would cry and talk about how lonely she was.

My mother wasn't the only person I saw attached to beings of this nature. I hated going out in public, because I saw so many of these discolored, mean, or unhappy beings in or around people. I recall seeing one on a cord that looked like a leash, attached to a woman at a department store. It looked like a lap dog panting behind her. I watched and was intrigued to notice that every time it "barked," she would plop clothing in her cart. I now think she had a shopping addiction that was reinforced by a bad entity.

A person may acquire one of these spirits from a parent, carry it in from a past life, or even unconsciously submit to it by participating in an addictive process. Freedom requires perceiving the presence of this entity; calling on divine help; figuring out if there's a "payoff," or benefit, for the attachment; and asking the Divine to take it to the heavenly spheres. Once this process is complete, I find the addict much more able to resist cravings and become self-responsible.

In my practice, I almost always see dark entities or energies attaching to people who have serious issues, especially addictions. Some of these dark entities are fallen angels who literally steal light from those they attach to. The victim, sensing a deficit of love and divine nourishment, becomes depressed and turns to false sources of fuel, such as alcohol, sex, or drugs. Other entities are passed down from an ancestor—or might be an ancestor that still preys on the living. I learned the power of these attachments in my own home. For three months, my younger son's father and I served as a halfway house for a loving and kind man who had just finished yet another round of chemical dependency treatment. Carlos had survived a shark-infested boat trip from Cuba to the United States when he was a child. His mother, brother, and others had died on that same boat trip. A professional athlete, he had won a bronze medal in one of the Olympic games and had become a strong Christian. Later, though, he slipped into a crack addiction.

He told me that there was a spirit that told him to take the crack. At the time, he was sober, and so I could not see the spirit with my clairvoyant eyes. Once he got a paying job, the money burned a hole in his pocket, and he immediately went out, bought crack, and got high.

The police found him on a ledge of a building, threatening suicide. Carlos told me that the spirit of the crack was a demon who insisted that he kill himself, or it would kill his son. While police intervention helped Carlos live to see another day, it could not cure the real problem. While his son survived, Carlos was still scared that the entity would eventually win. Eventually, Carlos learned that he simply couldn't use crack or any other substance.

I believe that the innocent of heart are often the most susceptible to these greedy and violent entities. I once spent two hours on the phone with a woman from Chicago who had allowed her ten-year-old son to play with a Ouija board. The Ouija board by itself isn't a problem, but previously, the boy had told the mother that a "dark angel" had asked to talk with him via the board. When the boy began the conversation with the board, the spirit apparently entered the boy, who was at the time of the phone call levitating and shouting obscenities. His mother and I performed an exorcism to free the boy from the demon.

Most cultures believe in otherworldly beings, although they use different names, including angels, demons, ghosts, Thunder Beings, kachinas, jinn, and fairies. I find it ironic, however, that so many Westerners still question the concept. No matter—whether or not we believe in them, *they* believe in *us*.

The human mind can bend—but it doesn't like to break. It can learn—but it doesn't like to. How many times do we need to see proof of the truth, proof of the supernatural, or proof of something even more important—the Divine—before we can accept what our eyes can see, externally and internally? How much longer before, as a species, we start believing our inner sight and our hearts?

THERE ARE MORE things in heaven and earth, Horatio, than are dreamt of in your philosophy.

—William Shakespeare,
*Hamlet*

# Divine Inspirations

There is a saying that you are not given more than you can handle.

I would like to argue that point, however, and I am actually angered by the notion that I can singlehand-edly deal with everything life hands me. The truth is that sometimes we are given more than we can handle so that we open ourselves to divine guidance.

I do the laundry and the dishes, the grocery shopping, and the bank and post office duties. I feed five animals and two children. I loved sharing my home with a friend's daughter for a few years, and I now cherish her son. I help my mother, who lives independently, and I see thirty clients a week, write books, teach classes, and travel for work. I also have a relationship with an intelligent, creative man. I have friends that I see for movies and chat with by phone or e-mail. By the end of the day, I am tired. Then it all starts over again in the morning.

I can handle the above. No doubt your days have a similar number of activities, frustrations, and rewards.

Remember the story of the smashed finger in the car door on the way to school? On days like these, I switch from the "I can handle it" mode to the "this is too much for me" setting. This is when I turn to the Divine for my source of inspiration and energy. At these times, I picture the Divine like a big generator. I am like this little pink bunny rabbit with batteries. When my own battery gets low, I plug into something stronger—and that something is the Divine. The Divine usually gives me pictures that tell me what to do—like taking the smashed-finger son to the hospital emergency room instead of making do with a bandage.

These everyday crises, however, are nothing compared to the tough stuff that life hands out: marriages, divorces, deaths, accidents, illness, and cruelty. While I have had faith in the Divine since I was a child, I believe that faith is not enough. Trust and action is also required, but not always our own action. We have to go a step further.

We are sometimes given *more* than we can handle so that we can ask the Divine to handle it for us.

This concept is the starting point for true growth. If we are to meet life's challenges and prosper, we must embrace a divine that is more than a god; we need the Divine to be a friend. Friends help each other. We need to stop worrying about whether or not we believe in the Divine, and instead lean into the Divine's belief in us. Moreover, we need to accept that there is not just one way to the Divine; one religion is not any better than another.

For me, my path is Christianity, more because that is the path the Divine chose for me rather than anything I have wanted for myself. Ironically, Christ is the one that enabled me to embrace all other paths.

## The Divine as Christ

Besides visiting my tea parties with angels, Christ would visit alone. I did not think of him as the Son of God, merely as a nice man who was pretty fun, kind of quiet, and a good storyteller.

I loved stories. I loved books and fairy tales—anything that started with "once upon a time." My mom would tell me customized versions of Peter Pan, and I would go to bed dressed like Wendy or Peter. Christ's stories were equally interesting but slightly more instructional.

Once he told me about a little star that fell to Earth and was shocked to discover that humans were stars who had also fallen from the heavens. Sometimes he would relay stories about the Holy Grail—not only the vessel but also the voices that composed it and formulated wisdom for humankind.

As I grew up, I learned about Jesus the Nazarene through the Norwegian Lutheran viewpoint. I went to church, sang in the church choir, and had fun with the youth group, but I was more than ready to turn away from Christianity when I was old enough to leave home. And I did. I was ready to explore other cultures' spiritual beliefs and religions, as well as my own gifts.

In my twenties, my clairvoyance, which had dimmed during my teen years, began to reawaken. I was driven to take classes internationally, in Venezuela, Belize, Costa Rica, Mexico, Peru, and other sites in Central and South America, as well as the Asian, African, and European continents. In Belize, I studied ancient plant medicine with shamans. In Mexico, I rented a car and took off across country, seeking a professor who had been studying shamanism.

In Peru, I imbibed sacred medicine to speak with the spirit teacher Pachamama. I once spent several nights alone in a thatched hut in the jungle as Pachamama taught me how to perform visioning. She started by showing me a light, which I was then instructed to expand into various shapes and pictures until, finally, I knew how to control light with my clairvoyance.

Inevitably, my cultural studies discussed the system that the particular culture used to interpret energy. I had already learned about chakras, which seem to have varying numbers of energy centers, depending on the culture or practice that discussed them. But my own searching led me to develop a more finely honed system of chakras and explanations of energy. I expressed these findings in my first book, *New Chakra Healing*, and in later books, and developed the Four Pathways system of healing, which organizes chakras for a multidimensional approach to change. I have continued to explore various ways to help people through energetics. But no matter which system

I purvey, explain, organize, or use, it all reduces to the nature of the Divine within—and without. Specifically, every experience has shown me that the Divine is in everything and everyone. The Divine looks at the world through our eyes.

A question emerged to which I began to devote my time and attention: if the Divine looks through my eyes, is it possible to see the world through the eyes of the Divine?

Ironically, I couldn't find the answer to this question until I returned to Christ, the source of my childhood religion.

## The Divine in All

Some years ago, I was chronically overworked. For a break, I used to drive to my "cabin" (real name: mobile home) up north (sixty miles away and slightly west, only a little north), mow the lawn, and come back home, all in one day. As intense as this may sound, there were therapeutic aspects.

I was driving back from the Cabin Up North at night when I experienced my first major divine visitation. First, a lightning bolt of white energy struck me, entering from the front right side of the car's windshield. It was so strong and blinding, I pulled over to the side of the road. A voice, which I call God's voice, spoke.

"You are loved."

My heart was beating so erratically, I couldn't think straight. Finally, I composed myself and began to drive again. I had only gone a few more miles when I experienced another shock.

Jesus suddenly entered my body from behind me.

I knew it was Jesus: I recognized him from my tea parties. His energy was smooth and loving, and I found myself sinking into it. Then, suddenly, the entire world before me turned white—not just the flat lands around the highway but the entirety of the earth. Once again, I pulled to the side of the road to embrace the full vision.

"This is how I see," he said. "Heaven is *on* earth."

I saw the beauty of this world and the goodness underneath it all. We don't have to—and aren't supposed to—wait to die before we experience divine grace. We are supposed to see, create, and enjoy it *right now*.

When he pulled out of me, I felt sad and a little scared. I knew it would take me a long time to see the world this way again, but that ultimately was my purpose in life.

Since that time, Christ has appeared to me several more times. The next time was as a full-body apparition. My father was dying of lung cancer, and I was in Wales with my friends Robert and Cathy. Every day, we would hunt down a telephone booth so I could call him. On the day of this appearance of Christ, I had already made my call, and we were exploring an old church on the coast.

I wandered alone to the nave and spied an old wooden cross. Then I began to cry for my father, whom I loved deeply, and for myself, because I would miss him. Christ walked out from the other side of the cross and held his palms before me. I could see the imprint of the nails on his wrists. He simply looked at me while I cried.

Christ was not going to "save" my father, either through healing him or convincing his soul to give itself to the Lutheran Church's idea of Christ. Jesus's gaze told me that my father was already saved, in that he was loved. Neither was Jesus about to erase my sadness, but he would cry with me—and he did, big tears flowing down his cheeks. The Divine can't lift life experiences from us, but it can accompany us on our walk through it.

The following summer, I was in Scotland with three good friends. We had a great time visiting sacred stones, eating out at pubs, and shopping. Our last adventure was a visit to a museum in Glasgow that featured the iconographic representations of all the world's religions.

There we were, gazing at statues of Buddha and Ganesh, portraits of Shiva and Shakti, prayer books to Allah and Jehovah, aboriginal artifacts, and images of the Catholic Mary. I was standing underneath a Salvador Dali picture depicting Jesus on a cross hanging over the world when Jesus taught me another lesson. He literally walked out of the picture and stood next to me. Finally, he whispered in my ear: "Isn't it wonderful, how many ways there are to worship God?"

Then he disappeared.

These visitations brought up many questions for me. Seeking answers, I enrolled in a Christian seminary to work toward a master's degree in divinity. I loved my studies but struggled with reactions from other students, who thought I was too "New Age." I didn't finish the degree, as I became pregnant with my second son and was too overwhelmed to "do it all." In all, I owe the experience a lot. I figured out that Christ can be learned about both in a classroom and out. Previously, I had discounted my experiential interactions and thought the only "true" path had to be validated by a church or a degree.

Every one of my clients has a different sense of the Divine. Some listen to the Divine via the mouth of a preacher, rabbi, priest, or spiritual director. Others meet the Divine in a place of worship; others see the Divine in their homes, on a walk, or in nature. To others, the Divine reaches out through a good book, a movie, or a tune on the radio. When all that we see is, in fact, the Divine, we no longer need to limit it to our own ideas of divinity.

## A Walk with God

Having accepted that I had my own way to relate to Christ, I was more than willing to let others explore their own relationships with the Divine. Personally, I was still confused about how to call upon the Divine in my personal and professional life.

I think most of us have struggled to define God or the Divine. Our tendency is to see the Divine in purely human terms. I have been pretty vocal to God about things that don't go "right." *Why did you send me here? Why did you give me these parents? Why don't you send help? Why should I believe in you, when you have obviously let the world go*

*to rot? Why should I believe you when you do not have a body?*
It's a good thing the Divine is patient, because I gave him
a workout on every level. I persevered in my cycle of listening to him, yelling at him, and listening again.

That pattern only broke a few years ago when I was in
England, teaching. I had just led a class in the Manchester
area and was laying down to sleep in a local bed-and-
breakfast. Just that evening, the innkeeper had been jok-
ing about the spirit that occupied the B&B. Apparently,
the spirit loved to pull pranks; once an entire breakfast
had disappeared, and no one had ever figured out where
it went. I was exhausted and fast asleep when, at some
point in the middle of the night, the bed began to shake.
"What?" I asked grumpily, figuring that it was the ghost.
There was no response, so I went back to sleep.

It happened again. This time I was not so nice.

"WHAT?" I demanded, but again, there was no answer.
Once more, I drifted off.

A few moments later, I was again awakened. By now, I
had no patience left—though I seldom have much anyway. I sat up. "Who are you, anyway?" I yelled.

I both heard and saw the answer.

"God," the voice said. There, on my right side, was a
male figure that looked like he'd stepped out of a kid's
superhero movie. He was entirely aflame in a bright red
fire.

I couldn't think of what to say, but my Norwegian
manners resumed. "Oops, sorry," I mumbled. I lay back in

bed, frozen in fear, and somehow eventually drifted back to sleep.

God as superhero remained with me for three more days. Although I could not see him with my physical eyes, as I had that evening, I felt his presence, imagined him in my mind's eye, and could hear his voice. He hung out with me. I was not quite sure what to do, so I talked with him as I would a friend.

A few days later, I flew home to Minneapolis from England via Iceland; God continued to accompany me. I was a little confused, for I was not sure where he would sit on the plane. I was sitting in the window seat, with an East Indian gentleman next to me on the aisle. Suddenly, the gentleman got up and took another seat. His seat cushion relaxed and smoothed out. I then heard God say: "Now I have a place to sit." The cushion indented and remained so during the entire ride. God continued to walk with me until I got home.

My first night home, he suddenly shifted form, from man to cloud. I felt the change instantly and began to cry. I wanted God to be a person, even if he was a little fiery looking. I began to doubt the entire experience, wondering if I had made it all up. Maybe it wasn't real? Maybe God wasn't real.

Then I understood. As children, we believe in what is concrete; we want tangible proof. We want God to be our mother, our father, or maybe our favorite dog or kitten. We only believe what we see and touch. For God to be all—for the Divine to be all of us—it needs to be invisible as well as visible, immaterial as well as material. Our child-minds and our immature aspects are unwilling to accept something as true based on faith alone.

So we create religions. If others see or describe God the way that we do, we have an easier time having faith. We carve God into pieces to suit our idea of reality and then expect that God meet our expectations, rather than the other way around. God as a cloud did not seem as concrete as God as a man.

Some time later, my son Gabe was playing in the living room with his friend Jacob. I was sitting in the corner, reading, when suddenly various objects began to fall over. First a lamp, then a book from the coffee table, and finally, the door blew open and knocked over a pile of magazines. Gabe did not even look up from his play, although Jacob asked, "What is that?"

"Oh, that's just God," replied Gabe, who then continued to kill off one action figure with another.

Silence hung in the room, and finally Jacob spoke.

"That doesn't happen in *my* house."

All I could think about was what would happen when *this* got out to the neighbors.

SOMEONE'S OPINION OF you does not
have to become your reality.

—Les Brown

# What the Neighbors Think:
## *Living as Who YOU Are*

One of the greatest challenges in being ourselves is being okay with what others think of us. This continues to be a life test for me and for many of my clients.

How have I, as a clairvoyant, determined how to *not* care about what the neighbors think—even while I care about the neighbors? It is an important issue for all of us.

As I have grown in my skills, gift, and practice, thanks to many wonderful and challenging clients, I began to realize that all the questions I heard reduced to three spheres: work, relationship, and health. Through these spheres, we experience all facets of life—as well as the Divine, growing and developing in relationship with this highest power and also with our own divine selves. Ultimately, the key to a successful life is to choose joy over dismay. And the key to joy? Understanding the divinity of being human—the kind and special human beings that we are.

Although we are supposed to become *who* we really are—the most unique self we can be—the world doesn't generally reward individualistic behavior.

One of my clients is a well-known physician. He put a sign up in his office that said "Prayer and Meditation Allowed." He had found that when he prayed with his clients, the surgery was more successful.

He did not force his clients to pray. He did not even limit the connection with the Divine to prayer; meditation, a more holistic concept, was perfectly acceptable to him. He simply provided the option. Although his patients loved him, the other surgeons felt threatened by this "non-standard" practice and forced him out of the clinic.

Yet another example was a ten-year-old boy who was a brilliant musician. He played the trumpet and had been asked to play a solo with an adult orchestra. He came to see me because he was upset to the point of not being able to play because the other kids at school called him "fish lips" and would steal his trumpet when he was not looking. Why would any of us want to be who we are supposed to be when it earns us the title of "fish lips"?

I thank the Divine that my special gift is as unique and odd as it is, for it's forced me to walk to a different drummer—to learn that I must accept myself for who I really am and only then consider others' opinions. In the end, personal integrity is the only measure that matters, although the path to this learning has been a painful one.

## Seeing Relationships for What They Are

We all want to be liked and accepted. Being a clairvoyant is one strike against you from the get-go.

I think my father was the most challenged by my gifts, probably because he had something to hide that was only discoverable through the invisible. I had a recurring dream throughout my childhood; finally, as a teenager, I took him out to dinner and asked for an explanation.

In the dream, I was a soul floating around an apartment. I could see a man and a woman. The man had blond hair, blue eyes, and big shoulders. The woman had brown hair, which was tied back in a kerchief, and a blue blouse. I knew that they were supposed to be my parents and that the man was my current father—but something was wrong.

The two were arguing about religion, and finally the woman stormed off, crying. I kept calling after her, but she shut the door and was gone. I turned to my father in the dream and tried to get him to go after her, but he couldn't hear me.

"She's pregnant!" I kept shouting. "She's pregnant!" But he couldn't hear me.

I had always felt like I had the wrong mother. I have grown to love and respect my mother and count her as a role model: she is a woman of learning and grace. Who am I to judge my earlier experiences with her, the challenging ones? I have certainly been a challenge to my own children; just ask them. Nonetheless, I used to pretend I was an orphan, because I felt like one.

As I told my father this dream, I watched for his reaction. He turned ghostly white and quiet, and after a while, he explained part of the dream.

"I was engaged before I met your mother," he said. "She and I lived together and broke up because she was

Catholic and I was Lutheran, and I didn't want to hurt my parents."

I asked if he had known that this previous fiancée was pregnant when they broke up. My dad denied that this was possible, so I asked more questions.

"Does she have children?" I pondered.

"Yes," he replied, describing her oldest son, who had blond hair, blue eyes, and loved to fly planes. Like you, I thought. I thought it interesting that his former fiancée married almost immediately after the breakup and had a child soon thereafter.

After that discussion, my father's attitude toward me shifted. Whereas before he treated me like I was odd, now he was both respectful *and* frightened of me.

I have found that men—especially those I could connect with romantically—are often anxious because of my gifts. I suspect they feel vulnerable and exposed, while I just want to be courted.

I feel compassion for my oldest son's father. When we met, I had no way to manage my gifts. They had just reawakened, and he experienced the results of my lack of control. I still remember getting out of bed one night in a huff, throwing open the window in the bed-and-breakfast we were staying in, and beginning to yell.

"That's it!" I proclaimed. "Your ex-wife keeps hanging around our room, and she's got to go!"

He thought I was crazy. I thought so, too.

His ex-wife's spirit was hanging around; I have found the living can "split" their souls into parts and leave an aspect in other places. As well, a soul journeys at night and often travels to other spaces—sometimes to haunt. In this instance, I also sensed the presence of a group of ghosts. Then there was his father's spirit in our living room. I had no idea how to stop seeing what I was seeing, much less control my gift.

Fortunately, I started to make friends with other "weird" people; I met them in healing or psychic development classes and other spiritual venues. I discovered that I was not as odd as I thought; other people were equally weird.

One of my new friends told me that she was awakened every night by a set of extraterrestrials who were teaching her the secrets of the universe. Consequently, she was always tired. Together, we decided that we might both benefit from psychic boundaries. She demanded a better class schedule from her nocturnal teachers, and I refused to talk to the beings that hung around me unless I thought they really had something to say. This conviction helped me translate the lessons about boundaries I was learning in therapy to the psychic dimensions, helping me filter harmful from helpful energies and set up parameters that cleared away the negative entities.

Even though I have developed stronger constraints, I'm still affected by boundary issues—that is, the lack of them in other people. For example, consider going to a party and saying that you are a psychic.

Often, people back away, as if I have announced that I have leprosy. People assume I am going to read their minds and discover all their terrible secrets, and maybe even say them aloud. I do not really care about the secrets that the partygoers may have. I hear these stories at work all day long. When I am at a party, I want to relax, have a glass of wine, and talk innocuous talk—you know, about the weather, movies, and the most trashy novels on the market.

A different party reaction is to turn me into the evening's parlor trick. "Oh, can you talk to my dead great-aunt Harriet?" For some reason, people commonly assume I walk around with a cell phone linked to the other side. Not only that, I have a super-duper dial-up plan and can link in anytime I want.

And of course, there is the area of predictions and prophecy. Stock market questions, lottery numbers, stocks, bonds—which ones? Truthfully, if I knew these answers, I'd be rich—and *not* at this party.

Sometimes, I become the color swatch of the universe. I actually do see people as colors; that is how I read their personalities. I spent one evening at a friend's family event sharing everyone's colors with them. It was fun, but I was exhausted and more than a little gray by the end of the evening.

And there's always the "true love" hunt, a setup if ever there was one. This is usually after someone "secretly" shares my profession with another partygoer. A man or woman will come over, begin with small talk, and then start in with their real questions: *I met my soul mate, and he broke up with me; is he going to return? Do you think I'll ever find true love? I just started dating this person; do you think it will work out?*

The hardest boundary-crash is when someone needs healing or wants the same for a loved one. Some parents actually thrust their terminally ill children in my faces, asking for a miracle. In Russia, England, and here in the United States, I can be mobbed for hours after a seminar. People will also try to follow me back to the hotel, always seeking information, insight, and healing. I do care, but I need my solitude in order to be the best clairvoyant I can.

Just a few months ago, I went to a local bed-and-breakfast for a break in order to do some writing. As soon as the owner discovered that I did healing work, she unloaded all her physical issues and complaints to me before asking her daughter-in-law to come over to do the same! I was there to work on a writing project; you can imagine how much I really was able to accomplish.

My real pet peeve, however, occurs when I run into a client when shopping or doing anything in public. I can't count how many times clients who assume that just because I get visions in private means that I can—or want to—do so in public. The most memorable time this happened, I was in PetSmart hoisting a thirty-pound bag of dog food while my nine-year-old son held onto the wild beast Honey, who in turn was simultaneously salivating at the cats up for adoption and striving to attack someone's miniature pet poodle, when a client ran into me and asked if she had just met her mate.

I don't remember what I said, but it was obviously something blunt; I've never heard from her again. Each of us likes to be valued for our work, but that is just one sphere in our lives. Remember the Golden Rule—treat others as you want to be treated yourself.

## Divine Retribution

Every once in a while, I decide that I'm not going to use my gift unless I'm with a client or absolutely forced into a corner. That is when the Divine shows me who is boss, and it is not me.

One day, I got up and told the Divine I was done working for him, at least for the day. No one called. I did not receive a single vision. I was relieved; I thought I was in the clear, as I headed off to Target with Gabriel. My only goal was to buy food, kid shoes, and throw pillows—especially the latter. When the wild dog ate the couch, he had also chewed up all the pillows.

The shopping took longer than I had hoped, and we were finally heading toward the checkout, well past dinnertime—having not eaten—when I heard a voice in my head: "Help that man."

I groaned. I confess—I ignored the voice. I knew who it was, so I did not answer. I was hungry and cranky, and it took all my energy to hold the pillows atop the mounded cart. Gabriel was doing his part too, whining and keeping me aware that he had not had dinner.

"Help that man."

I sighed. I knew I had to at least look at the object of the Divine's affection.

A man sat on the bench near me. He was young, had an empty stare to his face, and was rocking back and forth. I caught his eye.

"Lady, do you have any money?"

"No, I don't," I said, giving up. *Here we go,* I thought, *working again.* I saw a vision in my mind of this young man with a group of others; they had dumped him here with no money or contacts. Where was he from? I could see a forested area, but I had no idea where that might be.

He proceeded to tell me his story, which mirrored my intuitive assessment. He and his "friends" had driven in from Seattle. They had taken his car and left him at Target. He had sat on the bench all day, with no food or money. He couldn't even make a phone call. I called the manager over and requested help, soliciting a free meal from the restaurant manager, whom I knew. After about an hour, he left with the police, who took him to a shelter that would contact his parents.

The truth is that most of us like to use our gifts when we want to—when they serve and are convenient for us. It simply does not work that way. Our gifts link us with the Divine, and the Divine asks us to use them.

## The Inconvenient Parent

My gifts are perhaps least convenient for my children. Though they are pretty good at pretending they don't have a clue about what I do, they are actually very aware of my talents.

The father of my oldest son, Michael, is a PhD epidemiologist, known internationally in his field. His fundamental training, however, is in animal farm management. Essentially, he is a pig doctor. How would you feel if you had to tell people that your dad is a pig doctor and your mom is a psychic?

Lately, Michael, who is now a college student, declares that his career, whatever it will be, will certainly *not* be weird, like his mom's. He is majoring in journalism, with minors in English and religion—almost the same studies as I took in college. I've decided not to make a point of the obvious.

My youngest son, Gabe, puts up with what I do—so far. But pre-puberty has struck, and he's made the same declaration as his brother: "Mom, you're weird."

But times have changed. Years ago, Michael's teachers ignored me when I described my profession. Gabe's teachers are almost the opposite. One of them asked, "What do you do for a living?" When I told her, she said, "Cool"—and went on with the parent-teacher conference. That was refreshing for me.

Some people might think that parenting psychically gives me an edge; sometimes it does. Michael said once, "It's a drag having a psychic mother. I get caught at everything." The truth is that his stepmother, an incredible person, has uncovered equal amounts of wrongdoing. Mothering is simply an intuitive art.

Being psychic is also one of the most heart-wrenching and painful talents, even with the so-called upside of intuition. Take prescience. I can be extraordinarily accurate at predicting the future, but sometimes all I do is sense, not see, what is coming up—let alone the knowledge of when. A few years ago, I tossed and turned all night long, a pit growing in my stomach. Something bad was going to happen the next day. The only picture I could get was of my kids, but that was not enough for me to create a preventative plan.

In midafternoon, I received two phone calls at nearly the same time. Michael, who had just turned sixteen and received his driver's license, had been hit head-on by another car. The car he was driving was totaled, but he was okay. My youngest son had fallen at the playground and was bleeding and needed to go to the doctor right away.

Which child should I help? I ran outside, only to discover that three of my four tires were deflated. I had a relatively new vehicle, so this did not make any sense. I called a friend for help to pick up my youngest son. I called my oldest son's father to help Michael. A few hours later, I was sitting with both boys at Tires Plus, exhausted but grateful to have both boys sitting with me.

Did "God" want these events to occur? I hardly think the Divine would have sent an angel to slash my tires, sabotage Michael's driving, and push Gabriel off the swing set. Whatever the causes of and factors behind these two events, they were set in motion well before that moment, or I wouldn't have seen the pictures.

**IF PEOPLE BELIEVE** in themselves, it's amazing what they can accomplish.

—Sam Walton

# Part II

## Questions and Answers
### *What the Pictures Reveal*

Through my practice, I have concluded that my own life experiences are not vastly different from those of other people. We all grew up in dysfunctional homes. We have all been hurt and abused. We all have broken hearts, questionable relationship skills, and a sometimes-unexplainable faith in ourselves. We have all been blessed by others, scared financially, and injured physically. We agree that the world would be a better place if it would be peaceful—as would our lives. We simply need a structure for seeing situations clearly and determining how to handle them.

This need for a logical approach to our often-illogical lives has driven me to separate every life issue, dream, and problem into one of three spheres: relationship, work, and health. Try it. Think of a question that does not fit in one of these baskets.

Having an affair? *Relationship.*

Want to meet Mr./Ms. Right? *Relationship.*

Worried about the bills? *Work.*

Feeling unfulfilled? *Work.*

Not feeling well? *Health.*

Want more balance in your life? *Health.*

Even the Divine fits into a category—all of them. Our relationship with the Divine is the foundation for all other relationships, the kingpin for achieving our spiritual destiny, and the reason and means to embrace good health. When we conduct our life journey with the Divine, we make strides that increase joy in all three arenas simultaneously.

The rest of this book is devoted to analyzing these three life areas and addressing the most common situations that pertain to each. In chapter 6, I define terms. What is relationship? What is work? What is health? What would it look and feel like to be satisfied in each? In chapters 7 through 9, I present the most popular questions I hear as a clairvoyant in each of these three categories. Using a question and answer (Q&A) format, I follow each query with a response. The response demonstrates the answer I most often "see," or intuit. In many cases, I also include a short client story to clarify my response. In the conclusion, I leave you with one additional message—a benediction, really, for embracing your own intuitive gifts one picture, step, moment, or heartbeat at a time.

# 6

# The Three Spheres of Life

We all desire happy and fulfilling lives. Unfortunately, there is no formula for guaranteeing this outcome, even on a daily basis. I cannot count how many times I get up in the morning excited for the day and get that phone call that sinks my heart. Someone is ill. An important appointment was cancelled. The check is *not* in the mail.

At the same time, life can deliver some absolutely beautiful bouquets of flowers. The person behind you in line at the coffee shop offers to pay for your cup of tea when you realize that you left your wallet at home. You get to school and discover that your son is wearing the wrong color shirt, and in your car, miraculously, there is a sweatshirt of the correct color.

The down moments are more manageable—and the ups more apparent—when we separate life into three basic spheres of circumstance. What defines these three categories? How might life look if the circles' lines were unbroken and the space within the circles full? Who might we become if we could only embrace all parts of ourselves and become all of them at once? Let's find out.

## The Three Spheres of Life

In the esoteric world, a circle represents a beginning or starting point. A journey must begin somewhere. In life, it begins with the self—our essence, which is unique and eternal. We are born with everything we need to become great, but the abilities and dreams must be called forth. Life is only too willing to accommodate, and it does—by sending experiences that fall in three independent spheres of life that can be defined this way:

> **Relationship** is about connection.
>
> **Work** is about fulfilling our spiritual purpose.
>
> **Health** is about recognizing and
> living in wholeness.

To achieve our potential, we must be willing to see life as an odyssey and to view ourselves as the heroes in our own storyline. In my work as a clairvoyant, I often picture people as pilgrims who, as they walk their daily lives, come to crossroads. Here, they intersect with people, beings, or events that demand a response related to connection, spiritual purpose, or wholeness. It is not easy to be a hero. Sometimes we demand too much of ourselves, forgetting that even eagles start as hatchlings that first fly on wobbly wings. Even after we have learned to soar, a strong crosswind can blow in and send us back to the nest for cover.

If we can release the expectation of perfection, there is a good chance we can be satisfied in all three spheres of life. As a clairvoyant, one of my jobs is to tell people what is possible for them personally. One person's idea of relationship happiness might involve marriage, three children, and a picket fence. Another's inner wisdom might suggest a strong spiritual partnership with someone who loves to travel to Bali. We can get into trouble when we compare our lives with others. We can make the wrong decisions by looking at the Joneses and rejecting the choices that really reflect our true selves.

What does it look like to be in a "good relationship," have a successful career, or be healthy? The answer is personal, but the core criteria are the same.

## Satisfying Relationships

Relationships signify the bonds between our self, parts of our self, others, the "stuff" outside of us, nature, and the Divine. We need relationships with lots of people, beings, and places—including relatives, friends, acquaintances, business associates, spiritual guides, companion animals, the Divine, and even objects such as treasured mementoes. In general, we need to have the quantity and quality of relationships necessary to meet these seven intimacy needs:

- Mental stimulation
- Emotional closeness
- Spiritual development
- Value-based support, integral to the living of our values
- Physical nurturing, meaning sex or touch
- A sharing of passions, such as hobbies
- Unconditional love

I am constantly advising people on ways to get these needs met and ways to become a good friend to others, but overwhelmingly, the relationship most important and compelling to my clients is romantic partnership. It doesn't matter if someone is already married and is asking about his or her current spouse or is a single or divorced seeker, a five-time altar worshipper, homosexual, heterosexual, bisexual, asexual, or a sex-change recipient, or is young, older, or in between. The foremost concern in the relationship arena—and, in fact, in life itself—seems to be getting along with or finding one's "true love."

One client even came into my office with a ten-page printout from Match.com, the online dating service, to have me circle which of the many women might be his one and only.

Do I believe in true love? Yes, I do. I will explain further in chapter 7 on relationships. Do I think that we all have "the one"? Yes, although there are extenuating circumstances that might mean you will never be with your heart mate. Do I think we deserve true love, holy bliss, and nuptials that last forever? Yes, yes, and yes.

But let's be realistic. That, too, is part of my job. I can't offer hope if it is unrealistic. You wouldn't believe me, either.

The divorce rate in America is over 50 percent, and the only reason it is not higher is that people are tired of divorcing. They are either not marrying or not divorcing but still playing the field. Something is wrong with this picture.

I know what it is.

We are not starting at the center of the circle, the relationship with our *self*. We will never find our true mate or be satisfied with that person or any other until we are at one with our true self. To love ourselves requires ruthless honesty, impeccable self-acceptance, and the willingness to change.

Connecting the various parts of the self is not an easy job. We have many selves inside of ourselves. In general, I think there are three main types of selves: there are the shoulder guides, the time travelers, and the experience holders.

I learned about the shoulder guides when working with a pastor as a client. He could not decide if he should get divorced, even though he and his wife hated each other and had for years. They needed a good therapist, at the very least.

Over his shoulder, I pictured two tiny beings, representations of two parts of him. One was an angel with a halo. As you could imagine, it was chattering away with well-meaning advice to keep his marriage together. The other being was the shoulder devil, which, as I recall, was lounging on a Harley-Davidson motorcycle, taking a drag off a cigarette. The devil was having a wonderful time selecting Bible verses to torment the pastor's wife.

Another self I meet often in client sessions is the time traveler, the inner self that is either a child or an elder. Have you ever sat too long in a boring business meeting or a family dinner and been struck with the incessant desire to howl like a coyote? This is your inner child, who wants fun all the time. Sometimes it is great to let loose and let it out, but it is not cool when he or she kicks your boss in the shins just to see what might happen.

There is an elder time traveler, too, which is often a wise self. Sometimes this wisdom keeper is helpful; other times, it makes us stand out in a crowd, dissatisfied with our current reality. My oldest son exhibited this condition after I had picked him up from his first day at kindergarten. He said, "Mom, this is a total waste of time." Michael then pointed out that he already knew how to color, and it was only going to go downhill from there.

Finally, we have the experience holder. We learn from experience, but are we learning the right things? The healthy inner self makes appropriate conclusions. When someone is nasty, we can avoid him or her. If a job is not going to pay enough money, we do not have to take the job. The wounded experience holder, however, creates inaccurate conclusions and can completely mess up our lives. This is the inner self that might believe we deserve mistreatment and so keeps us taking inappropriate jobs with cruel bosses.

The major cause for relationship dissatisfaction lies with the wounded experience holder. I remember working with one client who kept marrying alcoholic women—five of them in a row, in fact. His mother had been an alcoholic, and his wounded self kept thinking that the next wife would love him enough to quit drinking—just like mother "should have."

We keep attracting what we are used to and fail to know what to do with it unless we face these inner issues. If we face this discomfort, we have the opportunity to be satisfied with ourselves no matter what is happening outside of ourselves. This is the key to inner peace.

## Satisfying Work

"Work" isn't a very satisfying word, is it? Roll the word on your tongue. It thuds. It is a hard word to swallow because of what it means in our culture.

Most of us link the word "work" with our paid jobs. And my clients do love to complain about their paid jobs. They do not like their bosses or coworkers, or they hate the work itself, or they feel bored or overworked or stressed, or they have to drive too far to get to their place of employment, or they miss their kids. Some people don't even realize they work or even "have" to work. Stay-at-home moms forget that every second of their career involves fashioning the next generation. It is easy to think that doing laundry or tending sniffling noses or volunteering for nonprofit organizations is less important than running a business meeting. And individuals endowed with trust funds often believe that their lives are unimportant, too. If you do not "need" to work, what's the point of life?

All the work complaints I hear reduce to one core concern: "work" is not a large enough container for one's destiny.

Most of us are too big for the box of most jobs. Work is a sphere, not a rectangle; no matter how hard we try to squeeze ourselves into the corners, some part of us spills out.

I had this image for the first time when a forty-five-year-old middle manager consulted me. He was bored. He felt stifled. He wanted to stretch his wings and fly.

I read his colors. Peoples' gifts can appear to me like a string of various colors placed inside or just outside of the body. Depending on the specifics of the color or their locations, I can determine someone's innate gifts and often the components of their true destiny—the reason they came to this planet for this lifetime experience. This destiny is carried in the spirit, the immortal self, which travels from lifetime to lifetime through the soul, the part of us that incarnates to learn lessons. Our destiny then locks into the body via our energy system, a complex set of energy bodies including the chakras and other energetic structures that manage our subtle energy. As I do with most first-time clients, I used my clairvoyance to examine this man's colors and advise him about future career steps.

Based on what I saw, I encouraged him to enter a partnership with a local health-club operator. He did. Within two years, he was a millionaire—and bored again. This time, I saw the picture of a basketball team and troubled teens. Two years after that, he was part owner of an internationally known basketball team and finally feeling fulfilled, not only because of his success and love of sports but because he was using his money to fund a mentorship program for juvenile delinquent boys. The colors I saw in his energy system were all being "used." Another way to express this is that every one of his spiritual gifts was being tapped to its extreme.

Work is not just about paid or unpaid jobs or even volunteer projects. It is about a way of life. We are here to live our destiny in all three spheres of life. No matter what our purpose—to heal, love, teach, create, illuminate, write, or simply share—our destiny is ultimately to be our true self. The key to living our purpose is to offer our gifts to others—the goal of work.

## Satisfying Health

When I bring up the word "health," most of my clients begin to turn red, shuffle their feet, or tap their pens. As a culture, we usually equate health with having a perfect body, internal and external, and we are often embarrassed about the behaviors that keep us from looking like Cindy Crawford or the most recent James Bond.

I once worked with an extremely beautiful woman who had spent ten years as a fashion model. At age twenty-six, she was bemoaning the fact that she had become "too ugly and fat" to continue her career. To my eye—indeed, probably to all those who saw her in non-work life—she was gorgeous. The profession had decreed that she was too old, however, and she believed it. In her point of view, she was therefore "not healthy."

She asked me what she needed to do to become healthier, and I saw two pictures. The first was a bucket of ice cream. The other was an image of a heart being hugged by two arms.

My client blanched. "I'm too fat because I eat ice cream all the time," she confessed. She lowered her eyes and then looked at me. "There are two images," I reminded her. "What's important is how they fit together."

I told her that the picture of the ice cream meant that she liked ice cream—nothing more or less. "Maybe it's good for you to eat food you enjoy," I suggested. I added that the image of the heart being hugged was the solution to her health problem. "If you can love yourself no matter what you look like," I instructed, "then you will be healthy. You will feel whole."

This former model *was* unhealthy—not in her body but in her mental state. She was afflicted with self-hatred and judgmentalism. There was nothing wrong with her body from an outsider's point of view, but she still wasn't a healthy person.

You cannot be healthy unless you accept and live from wholeness, no matter the state of your body—or, for that matter, all parts of you. Health is another word for wholeness. In turn, wholeness means holy. Our bodies are holy and sacred spaces for our spirit. Upon deciding to love all parts of our self, even those aspects and behaviors that we dislike or reject, our spirit can completely immerse into our bodies and we become transformational vehicles for the Divine.

Many clients feel less than whole because there is something "wrong" with them. I worked with a woman with diminished leg and arm function who is an artist. Injured in a car accident when she was a teenager, she was told she would never walk again and would be confined to a wheelchair her entire life. She refused to listen. She spent five years learning mind–body techniques and undergoing painful physical therapy to be able to use crutches and wield a fork. Not content, she spent another ten years in school learning how to paint at a level that has earned her world recognition. Her complaint, however, was that she did not "feel whole."

Healing can restore us to a previous state or can help us achieve an unknown state. However, it must encompass body, mind, and soul, as well as emotions, spirituality, and psychology, to lead to satisfaction. Someone with a lower IQ, such as a person with Down's syndrome, isn't a not-whole person. Someone with a mental illness or emotional problems isn't either. Quite simply, we have only to be the best we can be to be healthy.

Most of my clients are uncomfortable talking about their health concerns at first. As they become more comfortable with me, this changes. Approximately one-third of my clients call me for medical intuition work, in which I use my full faculties of intuition to sense a physical problem or the potential cause of a "dis-ease" and offer spiritual advice about how to address it.

I once worked with a woman who was "feeling funny." I saw white bubbles throughout her nervous system and suggested that she ask her doctor about lupus, an auto-immune disorder. She consulted the doctor, and the diagnosis was confirmed. Later, we worked on the causes, and she went into remission.

What helped her heal? I asked her body to take her into the situation that was playing out as a disease. She suddenly experienced herself as a man in World War I being mistreated in a concentration camp. As the story unfolded, she determined that the emotions from that experience had carried into her current body and were now causing the lupus symptoms. Forgiving the guards from that camp, she released the lupus. Her body had created the lupus to remind her that she was important enough to feel and express these feelings and return to a state of unconditional love. Having achieved this, the messenger—the lupus—could disappear.

I have found that many diseases or imbalances disappear or alleviate if we are able to uncover the message of love that lies underneath the appearing problem. Some diseases do not disappear, but we are better able to handle our physical challenges after examining other parts of the issue. In the end, wholeness is really about love—embracing the fact that we are loved, lovable, and here to love. Having said this, it is also important to lovingly and gently take responsible measures to be healthy. We do not have to be perfect, but it is really important to eat well, exercise, refrain from dangerous substances, and sleep. We can heal the past, but we must make changes in the present to create a desirable future.

It is not enough to uncover the causes of a problem; we must also live more holy lives in the present.

## The Center of the Spheres

What happens when we embrace our birthright for connection, purpose, and wholeness? We begin to live in the middle of the spheres.

In the center of the three circles of life is yet a different shape. Draw three concentric but interconnected circles and you will see what I mean. There, in the middle, is a fish shape. It is called the *vesica pisces*, and it represents the holy space, the place in which we meet the Divine.

Embarking on the journey of life is one thing; committing to it is another. Living our lives is yet another commitment to be who we are every day. If we are willing to be all that we can be in relationship, work, and health, we will find ourselves upheld by the Divine.

Here, in our picture, we have our very real and painful human concerns. But something magic and miraculous can happen: what has been disconnected becomes connected. Our limitations become our gifts. Our deficits become our new strengths. We find ourselves linked not only with the Divine but also with all of life. We find ourselves becoming more than we ever thought we could be, and it is good.

**TAKE AWAY LOVE,**
and our earth is a tomb.

—Robert Browning

# Q&A:
## *Relationships*

Relationships are about connection and ultimately about love. What are the most common questions I hear about love? What have I learned about love during my years as a clairvoyant? These are the provocative questions I address in this question-and-answer chapter about relationships.

This chapter is divided into several sections. It features topics such as love in general, true love, tough love, parenting, and the spirit realm, as well as some miscellaneous information.

### What is love?

Love is an energy, not an emotion, as is often thought. It cannot be measured, only described. As a clairvoyant, I see love as a shimmering rainbow of color; I discuss this further in one of the answers here.

Love is connection. It is invisible, though you can see when it's present or not.

There are many types of love. You have probably experienced most of them. We share one kind of love with our friends and another type with relatives, still different sorts with our coworkers, acquaintances, children, ex-mates, and lovers. All are love, because all involve connection.

## What is the purpose of love?

The purpose of love is to create authentic relationships. Authenticity means genuine. Authentic relationships provide the space for our own "genius," or genuine selves, to support the genius within others, and vice versa.

Love creates relationships, and relationships create love. There really isn't one that comes first; both blossom at the same time.

Think of the process that transforms a small bud into an exquisite flower. Cultivating the plant to produce buds and then flowers is not easy; neither is tending a relationship. The soil must be fertile and watered just enough, but not too much. It is equally important to balance sun and shade, to know when to prune, when to detach, and when to let the leaves go wild. In a human connection, acts of love nurture relationship in a similar way.

## What does a loving relationship look like to a clairvoyant?

I see loving relationships as shining with light. The greater the flow of light between people, the more loving the relationship. In the universe of a clairvoyant, love looks like a rainbow beam of light. Every color represents an aspect of love. When all colors are present in equal amounts, the love is pure and strong. If a color is missing, something is lacking in the relationship.

## What do the colors in the rainbow of love mean?

**Red** = passion

**Orange** = emotion

**Yellow** = intellect

**Green** = affection

**Blue** = communication

**Purple** = goals

**White** = spiritual connection

All these colors add up to human love. There is, however, a greater love: the love of the Divine.

When two people really love each other—when they connect through every color and the full spectrum of light—they also become conduits of divine love. The love they exchange between each other now begins to surround them and to spill over to others, inviting the Divine to be present in all they do.

## What is unconditional love?

We hear the phrase "unconditional love" a lot. What does it mean? Unconditional love speaks to a love or connection that persists despite any obstacles. Most parents unconditionally love their children, even when they are teenagers and the parents are gladly preparing for them to leave home. Unconditional love endures through anything life throws at us and shines through the veil of death. We could say that unconditional love is "inspired love," for it enables us to bring our spirit into ourselves and to help others do the same.

Conditional love is a form of love, but it is not complete. It cannot illuminate, nor does it inspire. Conditional love is more like a bargain. It is accompanied with an implicit understanding that fills in the blanks in this statement: "I'll give you _____ if you give me _____."

Conditional love does not form a connection; it creates a contract. If either side breaks the agreements of the contract, the "love" is broken. Conversely, unconditional love exists even if one or the other party breaks the conditions of a relationship agreement. For instance, two people might divorce because one cheated on the other. The terms of the relationship have been broken, and so the marriage is dissolved. The love is not necessarily destroyed, however. The connection can remain.

## Why is love so conditional on this planet?

Most of the complaints I hear about relationships come down to the difference between conditional and unconditional love. I hear various versions of these grievances, including the following:

- My spouse doesn't love me the way I want to be loved.
- I am not in love with my lover anymore.
- I don't love my parent the way I should.
- I can't seem to give my child what he or she needs.

The translation of the heart's yearning at the core of these questions is that we long for unconditional love and are not receiving it.

Another word for unconditional love is grace, which is the uninterrupted flow of divine love and power. During one particular session, I personally experienced the Divine's unconditional love so strongly that I will never doubt its existence.

My client was twenty years old and had terminal cancer. She did not ask to be cured; rather, she came to see me because she wanted an easy transition to the other side. She didn't want this for herself but rather for her parents, who had supported her throughout her treatment. About halfway into our session, the Divine spoke to us in a feminine voice. We both heard the same words.

"You are loved," stated the Divine, with so much conviction that I immediately began to cry. My client sobbed as well. We then heard a rush of noise and saw two angel wings, which enfolded my client in whiteness and light. The next day my client called. Her blood tests were normal. She had no indications of cancer, and it has never returned.

This divine love was clear and pure and asked for nothing in return. The Divine sought only to give, not to receive; to touch, not be touched.

Conditional love, in contrast, insists that you have to give "x" in order to get "y." The problem is that the people giving away "x" hardly ever get "y," but they lose "x" anyway.

This situation originates in past lives or childhood. At least 95 percent of my clients weren't loved unconditionally when they were young. They leave childhood with one of two relationship patterns: giver/taker or codependent victim/abuser.

These two roles show up in adulthood in a number of situations, including work and friendship, and usually in romantic liaisons.

Many people I have talked to assert that unconditional love is only possible when it comes from the Divine. I do not believe this. I have heard stories of remarkable love from human beings. However, we become what we have been raised to be. Because the world is full of givers and takers, we have very few models that can show us how to love unconditionally.

## Why would the Divine create a world with conditional love?

Our souls are here to experience love. They are also here to create more love—to bring light into the darkness and generate more heaven on earth. It is easy to be loving in a space that is unconditional—say, heaven. When all our needs are met and we know it, we don't have to stretch and grow. We become complacent. We don't actually have to be loving, because love is all around us. Neither do we feel stimulated to make more love than there already is.

We came to Earth because love is conditional here. That way, we get to ask ourselves this question every day:

*Will I choose to be unconditionally loving, even when surrounded by conditions?*

## How do I become more loving?

First, accept the love of the Divine. Second, love yourself. Third, love others. Fourth, give yourself permission to become a conduit of divine love. Fifth, forgive yourself and others for doing these steps imperfectly. Then start over again.

## I'm struggling to accept divine love.
## How do I make it easier?

Don't try. The Divine is capable of sharing love with you in whatever way you will be able to receive. Simply ask.

I had one client request divine love, and the next day, she received one hundred bouquets of white lilies; the florist couldn't track the order. These had been her deceased husband's favorite flowers. Yet another client asked the Divine to express love, and three cats showed up on her front door over the next week, needing homes. Who knows how the Divine will show you how deeply you are cared for?

# My One True Love

## Does everyone have a true love?

Congratulations! This is the single most asked question I hear as a clairvoyant. Here is my short answer: yes.

Here is the rest of the answer.

You have one true love in the spiritual sense. This love does not always measure up in the realistic sense. There is no universal law that insists that, in-body, you will meet or live out your life paired with your one true love. You may not even like him or her. Even if you both swear eternal love, there is no rulebook that forces the other person to take out the garbage, deliver breakfast in bed, or remember your anniversary.

We have all watched movies; even in the most adventurous films, there is a romantic pairing that happens. We old-fashioned romantics ignore the fact that Cary Grant, who almost always gets the woman in the film, really wanted men, or that Elizabeth Taylor and Zsa Zsa Gabor, actresses who always "got" their men, were never content with the ones they had. We think that true love mirrors the movies when, in fact, the movies reflect our fantasies about love.

In the supernatural world, a true love is called a spirit mate. Everyone has a spirit mate, a special someone that uniquely matches his or her own spirit. Your spirit is your essence, your true self. Back in heaven, you swam in the sea of the Divine's unconditional love until you emerged, ready to create more heaven on earth. In order to accomplish your goals, you partnered with another spirit—your spirit mate.

## Why is it so hard to find or attract my spirit mate or true love?

You and your spirit mate are ideally suited to support each other's destinies and exchange divine love. You can already see that life would be easier if you were with your spirit mate. Unfortunately, most spirit mates have become separated through the process of reincarnation and have difficulty finding each other.

I once worked with a man who had been married three times—to the same woman, although she was clothed in different bodies. Each wife was overbearing, nasty, and alcoholic. Every time he divorced, he vowed to find his *real* "true love." After the third divorce, he came to see me, wanting to uncover the problem.

My imagery suggested that his heart was closed to intimacy. Pictures revealed that his mother had not only been an alcoholic but had sexually abused him. The resulting shame and injury to his psyche made him think that he did not deserve true love, only an abusive situation. After healing his issues, my client began to visualize himself happy in a relationship. Within a month, he met the woman of his dreams. They moved from Minnesota to Hawaii and have been happily married for over ten years.

Sometimes we are not the problem in the relationship; the other person is. He or she might have more unworthiness issues than we do. I have a friend who knows her spirit mate. He has even acknowledged the same to her, telling her that he came into this life to be with her. Unfortunately, he is married to someone else. It is not a happy marriage, so logically divorce sounds like a solution. However, the man is frightened of real intimacy. At my suggestion—and her own common sense—my friend has moved on and met a different man.

Another reason for not meeting a mate is that he or she has not incarnated. I have a client who started crying nightly when she was fourteen. She came to see me at age thirty-four because she was still crying herself to sleep every night. As she explained, her "true love" never came to Earth. She remembers waving goodbye to him from heaven, sailing down to Earth, and awakening in a world he has yet to visit. That is 7,300 nights devoted to a spirit mate that isn't in-body.

Yet another reason for a missing love is timing. We might have decided to meet our true lover later, rather than earlier, in life. Personally, I had to fall down a few times before I could ride a bike, and my learning process around relationships has been equally challenging. Some of us simply are not ready for our true love until we (and the other) have matured.

To be truly partnered with your spirit mate is a beautiful thing. I worked with a couple that called each other a "heaven mate." They spent sixty years together. They had problems; she could not conceive, so they never had children. He was wounded in a war, afflicted with a leg problem, and later in life had arthritis. When Pablo died, Margot became very ill. I visited her in the hospital, where Margot smiled at me and squeezed my hand. "Pablo is here, next to me," she whispered. "Soon we'll be going home together." Margot died a couple of days later. Knowing that "heaven mates" do indeed exist can inspire us all.

### Is a soul mate the same as a spirit mate?

No. We have dozens, if not hundreds, of soul mates. Soul mates are members of our own soul family, which is a group of souls that reincarnate together repeatedly.

We come into life with the same soul group in order to help each other grow and evolve. Often we switch roles or even genders from lifetime to lifetime, depending on a life agreement.

My son Gabriel was my older brother in a different lifetime. When he was young, he kept asking if I remembered being his little sister. One of my clients recalls that his wife had been his mother in a different lifetime. The pattern established during that previous relationship continued into their current bond: she constantly bossed him around and he acted immature. What was the primary complaint she consulted me about? He didn't wash his own clothes. Despite her complaining, every evening she washed and pressed his dirty clothing.

## I don't think I've met my true love. How do I know I will?

The only one who can really answer this question is your-self—your own spirit. Use your intuition to reflect upon the question *Am I destined to meet my true love?* You might sense, feel, or know an answer. You might hear or see a response. You might get a resounding yes, a no, or perhaps a qualified maybe.

As stated in previous responses, most spirit mates enter our lives when we are ready. Before birth, many people set up several romantic relationships as precursors to true love. Each relationship teaches us something we need to know. These relationships invite us to face our issues, feel our unfelt feelings, and change our negative patterns.

These first relationships aren't always joyful or loving. They are lesson plans, which usually give us learning pains. For the most part, "true love" tends to present itself when we are self-aware, conscious of our own character defects as well as our spiritual beauty. Before awakening—before becoming self-responsible—most of us project our needi-ness or problems on our mates or, conversely, play the role of the caretaker, the one who has to fix it all. We have to break our own patterns to be truly in love and loving to other people.

My work has taught me that it is never too late to attract our true love. I once knew a couple that married at eighty. They had originally dated in high school. He joined the army, and she married when he was overseas. Each spent fifty years with someone else. Their spouses died within a week of each other—and this couple reunited within a month after that. They had been each other's spirit mates the entire time, but each had particular issues to deal with before they were ready to be really "in love."

## When will I meet my true love?

This is really the same question as the previous one, but I hear it all the time. I am going to give you the short answer: when you do.

If there is predestined timing, I can often sense a rendezvous with accuracy. There are still no guarantees; there is still human error, and there is still free will. I actually had one client yell at me because I said she would meet someone in three months—and it took four.

What causes the delays? We might not feel ready; we might not be ready. Perhaps one of the parties did not get a divorce on time or is not ever going to get a divorce.

Then again, sometimes everything lands perfectly in place. One of my favorite client experiences involves a woman named Janice, who hadn't had a significant romantic relationship for over ten years. Her job as the president of a company brought money and notoriety, but she was tired of sleeping alone, making meals for only herself, and taking solo vacations. She asked the age-old question, "When am I going to meet my true love?"

I saw an image, that of a man wearing pajamas, bedroom slippers, and an overcoat. To top it off, he had a mailbag over his shoulder. I groaned. I shared the image and waited for the eruption that was sure to follow.

"Is he a POSTAL WORKER?" she shouted in dismay.

"I don't know," I had to confess. "You'll have to see."

She left, disgruntled, and I couldn't blame her. Who wanted to marry a man who wears bedroom slippers with his overcoat?

Two days later Janice called, excited.

"Guess who I met?" she said. "The man of my dreams!" Janice proceeded to tell me that after our session, she had gone to her townhome's outdoor mailbox center, several individual mailboxes set in a circle. It was raining, so she had dashed out of her house with an umbrella. There she met her neighbor, who had moved in just a few weeks before. He had just flown in from Japan and was "off schedule" and taking a nap—wearing his pajamas—when he remembered that he had to check the mailbox for an important document. Throwing an overcoat over his pajamas, he had thrust his feet in slippers and run outside. The short end of the story was that he asked her out on a date.

A few months later, Janice left me an equally happy message. They were engaged; would I come to the wedding?

## Is there a way to meet my true love sooner rather than later?

The only way to hasten the meeting of a true love is to become the best person you can be. Why in the world would a true love pick someone who is unhealthy, addictive, needy, or desperate? I worked with one woman who was one hundred pounds overweight, hated her job, and whined all the time. She was mad at the Divine because she never met anyone. You don't have to be a clairvoyant to see that she was her own problem.

I worked with another man who, in his heavy gold chains and pressed Armani suit, kept cheating on all the women he dated. He could have already met his true love several times over, but he wasn't going to see that.

It is usually not worth finding a shortcut in the plan and starting a relationship prematurely. Sheila, another client, tried this—with detrimental results. In a session, I saw images depicting her true love that were so specific, I even provided his first name. I was told she was supposed to meet him in February. Our session was in August. She went home and demanded to meet him in November instead. She did.

This was the man. He had the predicted hair color and body build. He had the foreseen two children. He had just sold his business, as I had forecast. When intimate, he even placed his hand on her heart with the same tenderness the visions had suggested. Unfortunately, he was just ending a marriage. His moodiness created volatility between him and Sheila. The relationship did not work, and it is possible that rushed timing was a part of the cause.

### I've met my true love and it didn't work. Why not?

This happens. Sometimes our one true love says no, thank you, and leaves. Maybe we are the one that gets too scared or, in the end, sees that this is not for us and shuts the curtain.

We all have free will, even to the point of refusing a spirit mate. Spirit relationships are contracted in heaven; Earth is an entirely different environment. Mr. Z or Ms. A might have been perfect for us before he or she experienced the tragedies, traumas, and stresses of life, but the storms of reality might have injured him or her too much to honor the heavenly contract.

The most common scenario I encounter is that one (or both) spirit mate is too psychologically injured by life to engage in a true love relationship. No one contracts to be abused; nonetheless, most families have some dysfunction and are therefore abusive. No one establishes a life plan highlighting rape or mistreatment, but these are common experiences on this planet. The damage done to the psyche, body, and soul can prevent someone from becoming a truly available life partner. We must heal our wounds to become a capable true love.

## If my true love quits, can I get another?

There is a universal law, at least from my clairvoyant perspective: the person who shows up and tries, gets a prize.

The one who quits gets—well, not a prize; in fact, his or her next relationship will probably be difficult because of lessons not learned in the current situation. Things balance out, but not always in the way we want. This is not much consolation for the one who accepted the terms and conditions to be in the relationship at this particular time.

This means that if you are the one who really worked on the relationship and was left, the Divine will send you someone better. Better means capable and ready. If you are the one who failed to participate fully, you will attract a lower-level candidate and have to work your way back up. This is not punishment; it is education. When we are in school, we have to repeat a grade if we are not capable of the work to move on. We cannot progress unless we learn our lessons along the way.

I have seen this scenario play out repeatedly. A particular client comes to mind as an example. She was a lovely woman, kind and intelligent. She and her husband were deeply in love and had been married for a decade. The problem was that he kept having affairs—meaningless flings but hurtful to her. She begged him to get therapy, but he would not. She finally left him, certain she would never love again. Within a few years, she was married to one of the kindest, most amazing men I have ever met. Her former husband was still struggling to find love and was at that time in a relationship with a woman who kept cheating on him.

# Tough Love Situations

## I keep experiencing the same bad situation in relationships. What is going on?

Nearly everyone who walks into my office confesses that he or she keeps meeting, dating, marrying, or attracting the same person repeatedly—the new person simply occupies a different body.

A therapist would explain that this is a search for a missing or abusive parent. We attract what we are used to. Secretly, we think that this time, the new partner—who's really just a stand-in for our parent—will do it differently. This time we will be loved. Accepted. Not abandoned. This strategy is equivalent to telling a dog to be a cat and then becoming frustrated when it doesn't start meowing.

Therapists assess the psyche. I agree with the therapist's logic but would like to add a clairvoyant's perspective as well. We intuitively know that our parents are supposed to love us unconditionally. Love is an energy. It is a set of colors. If our parents can't share love, they don't send this rainbow of light into us—or all of it, anyway. We now have an empty space, an energetic hole. We seek people to fill this hole.

Unfortunately, we are not sending the right energetic message necessary to find someone who can fill the hole. Rather, our psychic communication attracts people that lack the energy—the love—that we really need. In other words, we are each missing the same ray of the rainbow. The empty space stays empty, and we feel even more unlovable.

### How can I break a bad relationship pattern?

The only way to stop your negative patterns is to find and fill the holes inside of you. Then you will stop looking for people to fulfill you.

The cause of a bad relationship pattern lies in the past, but the solution is in the present.

There are many types of damaging relationships; however, there are only two roles played in any relationship drama: victim and abuser. You know which side of the fence you play on. To renounce your role, you have to determine why you took it on. That takes a journey into the past.

I help clients accomplish this goal through regressions, which involve entering a slight trance state to return to a past event.

An example was a physician I once worked with who struggled with severe alcoholism. When drunk, he picked up women in bars. He had been married three times; his former wives matured through each of their relationships with him. They each decided that they deserved to be treated better. He did not understand the lesson.

I regressed this man into his past. Suddenly, he was age four again, and his mother, who was drunk, was having sex with a man in front of him. Apparently, she did this frequently. Her flagrant disrespect of her son taught him that he did not deserve self-respect. Angry, he decided to hurt women—any woman—as retaliation against his mother. During our session, the Divine literally walked into the scene, picked up my client (his four-year-old self), and saved him from his mother.

My client began to sob. For the first time, he experienced the Divine as real and felt himself as deserving of care, including self-care. The Divine had "plugged up the holes" and provided a new belief system upon which this man could now structure his relationships.

During his next visit, my client explained that he had stopped cruising the bars and drinking. I strongly suggested that he attend Alcoholics Anonymous (AA), even though he felt so much better. He wondered why, since he had just been healed. I explained that his child-self was now whole but that his adult self didn't have healthy patterns yet, which AA would help him establish. "You need to show your inner child that you're willing to treat him better than your mother treated you," I explained. He understood me and is now happily married to his fourth wife, a marvelous woman, and still attending AA meetings.

## What is an abusive relationship from a clairvoyant point of view?

A therapist defines an abusive relationship as one in which one or all members are being used sexually, physically, mentally, or emotionally, or are neglected. A clairvoyant sees abuse as the "stealing of energy," in which at least one member of a relationship or group is literally sucking the lifeblood out of another. The abuser is the taker, the thief of this life energy.

### What is codependency or victimhood from a clairvoyant point of view?

A therapist would suggest that a codependent, or the victim in a bad relationship, is the one who "gives away" his or her energy to the other. The classic scenario is the alcoholic relationship, in which the alcoholic makes liquor his or her god and the codependent turns the alcoholic into his or her god.

As a clairvoyant, I describe the codependent as the giver, the person who gives away his or her energy in order to feel safe.

### If someone knows he or she is abusive, how come he or she doesn't just stop?

People have a hard time ending abusive actions, including addictions, because of shame and because it is familiar. Many times they do not have an example to follow in order to make this change or have not consulted a counselor to begin this path.

From a clairvoyant point of view, shame is a gray, murky energy. It feels like a feeling, but it is not. It is like glue and sticks to beliefs that make us feel worthless, envious, bad about ourselves, and powerless. Abuse of any sort creates more shame; the more shame we have, the worse we feel about ourselves and the less willing we are to face the issues that bind us. In short, the more abusive we become, the more shame we accrue and the less we believe that we deserve to feel better.

Abuse can be self- or other-administered. Examples of self-abuse include over- or undereating, or obsessive-compulsive disorders including repetitive worry, selecting or staying in a negative relationship or system (such as a fundamentalist religion), or accepting less than we deserve. Addictions are often self-abusive as they involve hurting one's body, mind, and soul.

Many addictions, however, involve hurting other people, as well as oneself. These addictions include alcoholism or any other substance addiction and sex addiction. Abuse, including injuring others through sexual, physical, emotional, verbal, or mental violence, becomes addictive if it is repetitive.

## What must we do to stop abusive patterns?

In order to stop abusive and addictive patterns, we need to be willing to take the following four steps:

1.  Admit we have been wrong. More than any other reason, people refuse to change because they would have to admit they have been doing things the wrong way. The initial feeling of shame can be overwhelming.

2. Be okay with failing. If we have been abusive or addictive, we have obviously failed at being loving. Failing doesn't make us a failure.

3. Be willing to be banished. We might want to change, but this doesn't mean that others want us to change. They might not want anything to do with us once we get healthy.

4. Be willing to embrace the shame with unconditional love. Love heals shame. By loving the "bad parts" of ourselves, we free them from the worthless beliefs that are encouraging them to hurt self or others.

## What's the cure for the abusive relationship, for both the abuser (taker) and the codependent (giver)?

Abusers must stop stealing energy and start living from their true selves. To accomplish this goal, they first need to "plug into" the Divine, not the codependent or an addictive substance or a stimulating behavior. Once an abuser makes the switch, the real work starts, involving feeling the pain that has been hidden underneath the abusive behavior. Feeling this pain will lead to peace.

Codependents need to realize that pain and suffering is a birthright. No one has a right to stop another person from feeling his or her pain. By refusing to "fuel" the abuser, the codependent, or giver, can allow the abuser to feel his or her own feelings. In return, the codependent is able to enjoy his or her own life.

## How do past lives affect a relationship?

We have all been in relationships with the same people in several lifetimes. If we have had an encouraging relationship with someone in a past life, it will be a positive relationship now. The opposite is also true.

I once worked with a teenage girl who hated her mother. This is a common occurrence. It is called being a teenager, and the only cure for most of the symptoms is time. This teenager's situation was more dramatic in that she really did want to kill her mom, Sadie—and had almost tried.

I performed a regression with the daughter, Angela. We found ourselves in the 1500s, where Angela was Sadie's daughter, as she was in the present. In this lifetime, however, Sadie killed Angela with a knife because she found the girl in bed with her husband, who was Angela's current stepfather.

Sadie, in this current lifetime, had divorced Angela's birth father and remarried. After our regression, Angela broke down in sobs, admitting that her current stepfather had been sexually abusing her. She was mad at her mother for not figuring it out. We called Sadie into the session. She was shocked to hear the story. This time around, Sadie reacted appropriately. She called the police, filed charges against her husband, and took her daughter into therapy.

Past lives can affect even our non-intimate relationships, as well. I worked with a couple who lived in an expensive neighborhood. But their next-door neighbor was a sociopath. He shot gas bombs and BB pellets through their front window and left animal feces on their doorstep. He told the other neighbors that if they help helped my clients, he would murder them. And worse, the city would not prosecute the obvious felon.

When psychically reading the situation, I envisioned two lovely African American people living in a small Southern town in the 1930s. The husband had defended an elderly African American against a white person, and the Ku Klux Klan was not happy about it. Klan members burned a triple K on their front lawn, killed their son, and threw gas bombs through the windows.

My clients had returned to a new stage with the same script. The Klan leader of yesterday was today's sociopath neighbor. The government was irresponsible in both time periods. This time around, the solution involved calling upon loved ones and friends outside of the neighborhood to force the city to become responsible.

### How do I "let go" if I have been left?

You know how much it hurts. It is hard to be rejected.

If someone has deserted you, you probably had an intuitive inkling long before the breakup occurred but ignored it. If you really want to get over this hurt, there are a number of steps you have to take:

1. Make a physical change. Get the other person out of the house or get yourself out of the house. This means not only your house or apartment, but as a clairvoyant, I also help people release

others' energies out of their body. We are made of energy. Over time, the colors and auric fields of two people interact and merge. As long as we are connected, we will continually think about the other person—sometimes to the point of obsession. Spend time in prayer and meditation, asking the Divine to release the other's energy fully from your body.

2. Be responsible about your part in the relationship. Ask the tough questions. Did you drive the other person away? Was his or her behavior really a secret, or was there a hidden benefit in ignoring the bad behaviors? What did you get out of remaining in a bad relationship? Had you been paying attention to your mate's needs, or had your ardor and kindness evaporated long ago? We cannot move on until we look at the role we played in ending a relationship.

3. Grieve. A therapist will tell you to get out of denial and start feeling. Cry, get angry, move through the depression, and then accept the new state of affairs. That is important, but I add another level of grieving to my client's list of tasks: it is vital to grieve for what did *not* happen, too.

   We engage in a relationship because we have a dream. At some point, we believed that the now-defunct relationship was our dream. We thought the relationship was going to do something for us; we never thought it was going to do something to us.

4. Spin new wishes. On an energetic level, you never lost your dreams. They are still hidden in your heart, in an area I call the "dream chest." Spend time reopening this treasure chest, and set new goals for your next relationships.

## What actually keeps us connected to a former lover?

Much of my work involves helping the lovesick let go of "cords," energetic contracts that keep us stuck to someone else. Cords psychically look like garden hoses that run between two or more people.

Energy runs through these cords, often at a great cost to both parties. For instance, we might send someone our life energy in exchange for financial security. We might be tired all the time, and our partner might be resentful. Or we could give away our willpower so we don't have to work. We become the resentful partner and the other, overburdened. No matter how great the contract first seems, these restrictions limit love and hurt everyone involved.

Sometimes one party lets go of a cord but the other does not. For example, one of my Russian clients was sure that her ex-husband was her one and only love. She was devastated when he left her for another woman. Three years later, she was still fantasizing about his return—even though he had remarried and his new wife was pregnant. I saw a gray cord coming from her heart.

Her former husband kept batting the cord away. He was done. As soon as he rejected it, however, she shot it back at him. I knew my client was looking for a connection other than one with her former husband, and so we dug deeper. She admitted that her ex-husband reminded her of her father. Having never bonded with her father, she was intent on forcing a link to her ex-husband. We asked the Divine to detach the cord. Immediately, she stopped obsessing about her ex-husband. She was now aware of the real issue: a "hole in her heart," an emptiness that should have been filled by her father's love. After grieving this missing relationship, she began to find healthy ways to fill the gap, such as getting closer to male friends and treating herself with care.

## Is there a spiritual point to a bad relationship?

I had one client ask me this question after enduring a string of abusive relationships. The answer that came through me is that there are lessons in every relationship. Through divine healing and inspiration, we can look for the silver lining in every thundercloud and do something wonderful with it. But the following experience brings a framework to this question.

I was working with a pastor who was struggling with his faith. He had been professionally assisting a devout woman in his congregation who had spent fifty years with an abusive husband. For years, the pastor and his client had been praying for the salvation of her husband's soul. For the husband's part, he continued to cheat on his wife and indulge in too much liquor. Then the husband became terminally ill. Just before he died, he "gave his soul" to Christ. The pastor wanted to know why God waited so long to awaken the husband.

The only image in my mind was of Christ crying. I shared this with the pastor. "Does this mean that Christ is sad because the husband lost so much of his life to his sinful ways?" asked the pastor.

I heard words in my head and spoke them. "No," I replied slowly. "Christ is sad because the woman lost so much of her life to an abusive relationship."

## Do we pre-plan abuse? Does the Divine condone it?

Abuse is wrong. Rape is wrong. Incest is wrong. Cruelty is wrong. The Divine condones none of these. These have no part in any divine plan.

However, a soul sometimes preselects an abusive situation because it believes that will be the quickest way to learn a set of lessons. Other times, a soul allows abuse (or becomes abusive) because it becomes stuck in a pattern. We never need to feel guilty about being abused; we do, however, have to take the steps to heal from it and change.

## Does the Divine condone divorce?

I'm going to answer this question with a client story.

Francesca had been married for over ten years. She was a faithful Catholic, like her husband, and was the mother of two children. Francesca hated her husband.

He drank. He smoked marijuana whenever he was out of town. She was also sure that he was unfaithful, even though he was very demanding of sex from her. Worst of all, she suspected him of sexually abusing one of their daughters.

Her priest insisted that God did not sanction divorce; instead, she needed to keep praying for her husband. I looked at her and guessed the following. "You seem like an intelligent woman. You must feel guilty about something to remain in such an abusive relationship and to allow your daughter to be abused."

She started to cry; Francesca thought she was a bad person because she smoked.

I saw a picture in my head—God in jeans and a t-shirt, with a package of smokes in his breast pocket. I turned it into an assignment.

"Every day, after the kids have gone to school, I want you to make two cups of coffee. Put one in front of you and set the other one across the table. Now take two cigarettes and light them both. Smoke one and set the other on an ashtray near the opposite cup of coffee. That's God's coffee and cigarette. Now talk to God. Have a conversation—and listen."

She thought I was crazy.

She left and called a few weeks later. "I did what you said," she said excitedly, "and God talked back!"

"That's great," I said. "What did he tell you to do?"

"Leave," she said. And she did.

Would God sanction abuse? If not, why do we?

## Is it wrong to have an affair?

I have met thousands of people who have had or are having an affair. They usually enter my office with the same look on their faces, their eyes downcast, the shame literally dripping off their bodies. They clear their throats frequently. I ask if they are married, then we head one of two directions. Either I ask them to tell me about the "other person" or they finally say, "There's someone else."

I acknowledge that it is not my right nor anyone else's to decree that an affair is good or bad. In fact, from my perspective, a synthesis of twenty-plus years of working with clients in these situations, I have observed that there are beneficial affairs and harmful affairs.

Beneficial affairs occur when a marriage or partnership is already dead. In this case, at least one of the partners ends up with such low self-esteem that he or she does not have the energy to end the relationship, even if he or she wanted to. In this case, the "cheater" often enters a love affair in order to regain a sense of confidence and self-love.

An example is a famous lawyer with whom I worked during a time he was having an affair that did break up his marriage. The marriage had been bad for over twenty years, and he remained in it for the sake of the children. Since the birth of their first child, his wife had spent most of her time drinking in bed. A nanny had raised their children. Every time he suggested divorce, his wife tried to commit suicide. Regardless of what he did or said, the wife refused therapy or help for her depression.

Finally, my client met a lovely woman at work. Their affair started out as friendship and ended up in bed, he said, although they had recently ended the sexual relationship so he could make a decision about his marriage. He wanted to divorce his wife and marry his lover. Through our work together, he projected into the future, seeing nothing but pain if he continued the marriage.

My client filed for divorce, and the wife became suddenly invigorated. She called all his clients and told them he had been having an affair. She went after him with a knife and took the children, insisting that he would never see them again. My client persevered, however, and is now living with the woman he fell in love with and is at peace in his life. Through legal proceedings, he now has his children half the time. Was he wrong to have an affair? Quite simply, my client did not even know he deserved love before the extramarital relationship. True love made him truthful.

There are also harmful affairs. These are not about love. These are about power. They usually involve a string of short-term sexual flings by the cheater and are a sign of the cheater's inner turmoil, not a desire for the healing energy of love. While the partnership or marriage might be bad, this kind of behavior indicates an unwillingness to face internal or personal issues.

From a clairvoyant point of view, a harmful affair is an abusive/codependent (taker/giver) relationship. The "other" woman or man has become the gas tank for the cheater and is drained dry. There is not a two-way exchange of energy. Alcohol, drugs, and bars are often part of the scenery, as they empower the cheater to feel brave enough to injure self and others.

I worked with a man who had been cheating on his wife for years. To his credit, he did not blame her. He said he liked the thrill of picking up a woman, leading her on, and then getting rid of her. Working together, we uncovered severe abuse as a child. Neither of his parents gave him any attention. His father constantly indulged in affairs, and his mother was completely absent emotionally. She had never attended a single event he had been in at school. My client's payback for being hurt and ignored was to do the same to others.

## Why are there so many divorces right now?

We are collectively refusing to put up with abusive or negative relationships. This is a good thing. The difficulty is that we do not have a new model, in which everyone involved—partners and children alike—are treated with kindness and respect. Perhaps, over time, we will learn that marriage is not supposed to be a jail sentence.

# Parenting

## Do we pick our parents before birth?

I have two answers to this question, both equally true: yes and no.

Yes, we select our parents before birth, at least most of the time. We do this in an area of heaven called the "white zone," associating with our spiritual guides, others' souls, and sometimes even the Divine to make our future plans. We also choose many of our primary relationships and select "destiny points," situations that need to happen if we are to achieve our life purpose and heal our soul's issues.

We choose relationships and activities that will help us evolve. As stated in earlier answers, our souls, which have been incarnated before, carry wounds. Consequently, we usually select parents whose problems re-create our misperceptions so that we can reexamine the issues and hopefully come to a different conclusion.

There are a lot of pitfalls in the process. For one, we cannot force a potential parent to marry another potential parent. We might end up with one "right" parent and one "wrong" one.

There is also chaos. Let's say we're aiming for Paris but that "perfect mom" aborts us or is accidentally killed by a drunk driver. We now have to veer off to a different hosting womb in Hong Kong or Bangladesh.

Sometimes we take what we can get, just to be born or get close to the desirable plan. One of my clients, for instance, never felt like he fit in his family. He was the oddball, an artist in a clan of doctors. Why did he end up in these circumstances? They had the money to assure a good education. He had put his personal destiny before his desire for love.

## Do our children select us before birth?

In the same way that we choose our parents before birth, our children select us too. Usually we have incarnated with them before, but not always in the same family configuration. Our child today might have been our parent in another time.

## Why would my children have chosen me?

The good thing about being a parent is that you are usually matched with children who are wiser than you are. Parents think that parents are supposed to teach children, but in actuality, it is the other way around.

My son Gabriel reflected this wisdom from an early age. I asked him what I had done to deserve the gift of him, and he laughed.

"Mom, I came here because I was supposed to."

"Oh?" I asked. "Do you know the reason?"

Gabriel rolled his eyes. "Well, obviously, it's to help you. I am pretty smart, you know."

Then he laughed and returned to pretending to be a Power Ranger who needed to tie the dog's tail to the curtain.

## I cannot get pregnant. Is there some reason for this?

Sometimes we can't get pregnant for a simple physical reason. Not everything that occurs has a deeper spiritual meaning. My eldest son, Michael, summed it up years ago, when he was ill.

"Why do you think you don't feel well, Michael?" I asked.

He looked at me askance and replied, "I have a cold, Mom. Sometimes a cold is a cold."

Other times there *are* metaphysical reasons for fertility problems. Perhaps our soul decided not to parent during this lifetime. I have several friends who never had children; from an early age, they knew that they were not going to ever have children. Unfortunately, some people decided to skip parenting and do not remember this soul decision. For them, not having children can be agonizing. I once worked with one man whose sperm count was too low to fertilize an egg. We regressed him to the "white zone," the place of pre-birth decisions, and he recalled the decision to remain childless. He thought if he had children, he could not fulfill his life purpose. He changed his soul contract, and within a year, with no external interventions, his wife was pregnant with their first child.

Yet other times there are interference patterns, or entities, that prevent conception. These entities are usually souls (ghosts) from the family that, for some reason, do not want another soul incarnated. They literally position themselves outside of the living person's energy field and push away the baby souls. I worked on a woman who knew that a family entity was preventing a pregnancy; she could hear the voice of her would-be baby asking for help. We requested a healing from the Divine for the intruding entity. She became pregnant within a month.

## What does the mother-child bond look like from a clairvoyant point of view?

There is an amazing energetic bond that is equivalent to the physical umbilical cord. I call it the "umbilical bond," and it connects a mother to a child from the in-uterus period to three years of age.

This energetic cord allows the mother to sense and feel what is happening within her child. A thousand miles away, she can still tune into her baby's needs. On its side, the child can pull emotional nourishment and life energy from the mother. This beautiful system keeps both linked through a child's early years, the key period for psychological and physical development.

The umbilical bond first begins to disintegrate when the child is six months old. The next big shift occurs at eighteen months. The cord finally falls away at three years of age, leaving Mom ready to resume her own life and inviting the child to develop his or her own unique personality.

At each crossroads, the mother's energy suddenly pops open and is more available for her own life. If a mother releases this umbilical bond with love and acceptance, she often experiences the opening of new spiritual gifts and talents.

I worked with one mother who was able to paint as soon as her child turned three years old. Yet another mom showed a sudden interest in accounting, whereas she had previously been a social worker. Children bestow so many gifts; who would have known that they could activate our own?

## What happens if the umbilical bond does not disintegrate?

Sometimes the mother never releases the bond, which leaves both her and the child at a disadvantage for life. This might happen for several reasons. A mother might release her child to adoptive parents but miss her baby so much that she never liberates the bond. (See questions on adoption later in this chapter.) The mother might hate her husband or be single and thus psychologically make her child the center of her life. She might be scared of going back to work; if the child "always needs her," she won't have to. (These mothers often continue to have several more children so they don't have to face their own work fears.)

If the umbilical bond is not released, the mother and child form a dependency that can cause significant damage to both. The original love connection becomes a linked chain. Children are supposed to grow up and move away, establishing their own lives. If they believe they owe their mother their loyalty, they never individuate. They often develop severe abandonment issues and insecurities and do not know how to think independently. Mothers must eventually recommit to their own lives or else they fail to achieve their own spiritual destiny. If mothers overconnect to a child, they also are not available for their own personal relationships.

As a child ages, energy flows between the bonded parties, often producing startling results. I worked with one child with fifteen diseases. The mother used his illnesses as an excuse to stay home, even though the family needed her to bring in income. After releasing the cord, the child became well. Instantly. The mother spun into a severe clinical depression before beginning to deal with the real issue, her fear of failing in the "big bad world."

If the umbilical bond is not released, this cord is always present, regardless of whether the individuals know each other. I once worked with an adopted child who got the flu every two months. When he was thirty, he traced his biological mother and met her. She also got the flu every two months. The umbilical bond was still present, and through it, my client was receiving the only energy he could get from his birth mom: her illnesses. Upon releasing the cord, he stopped getting the flu.

### What does the father-child bond look like from a clairvoyant point of view?

The umbilical bond connects the mother and the child, but a father is not omitted from bonding to the child. His is a vital and sensational love.

A loving father will have established a strong heart bond between himself and the mother. He nurtures her; she nurtures the child. He is also connected to the child, often through a beam of light that connects to the umbilical bond. It forms a sort of tributary system to fuel the river of love between the child and the mother.

If the mother dies during childbirth or while the child is young, the father usually takes over the mother's role. The umbilical bond switches from the mother to him. If his grief is too deep, however, this transference never occurs and the child remains stuck in a state of detachment with neither parent present.

## What if I don't feel like I have bonded with one of my children?

Sometimes a child is born to us whom we have never known. We have experienced no past lives together. These scenarios can make it difficult to bond. They also provide the opportunity to expand our consciousness and grow a "bigger heart."

For some reason, we might not have established an umbilical bond or, in the case of the father, attached to the one between mother and child. A similar bond can be created at any age in the form of a rainbow light that can link our heart with that of the child.

## What kind of bond did Christ have with his parents?

This is a great question, one of the favorite ones I have heard over the years. So many Christians emphasize the bond between Jesus Christ and his unearthly father, considered to be God, that they fail to pay attention to the fact that he had a flesh-and-blood mother.

It is *impossible* for a child to become a healthy human being—to truly insert the "kind" in the goal of "humankind"—unless there is a linkage between the self and the mother, or years of therapy after the fact, in order to heal and compensate. During our early years, we can only really know our father through our mother. Personally, I think the Christian faith would be better served concentrating on the importance of the mother-child relationship and raising women to the standard of human beings on par with men, rather than worrying about how Jesus related to his father.

My attitude partially comes from spending years with a born-again husband. I was dismayed to hear the ridiculous reasons given to women, who were constantly told to submit to their husbands. This attitude is prevalent in most of the world's major religions, not only Christianity. One of the main rationales is that men are more like God the Father, and therefore better able to connect with the Divine inside as well as God's guidance. This assessment completely ignores the fact that the Holy Spirit named in the Old Testament is feminine and an equal part of the

Christian Trinity. As well, Christ could never have become the man he was, lacking a mother capable of defying tradition, following her intuition, and remaining strong in the face of condemning male authority.

During a relationship support group, the male and female married leaders encouraged the attendees always to follow the man's lead. I asked what should happen if the man were abusive and hurting the wife or the children. I was told that the wife should simply pray for God to change the man's heart. I pointed out that the wife had most likely been doing this, and if it hadn't worked yet, why would it at any point soon?

Religion is one of the main reasons that we hurt each other on this planet. I look forward to the day it might become one of the main vehicles for peace and love.

## I aborted a child. Am I guilty of an unforgivable sin?

You cannot kill a soul. Put aside the idea that abortion spins a child's soul into hell or purgatory, or that an abortion condemns your own soul to the equivalent state. The Divine is about grace, not accusation.

From my clairvoyant perspective, a child's soul does not usually enter the womb until at least the fifth month of pregnancy. Before then, it is usually still in heaven, although it might visit occasionally in order to meet the main characters of its upcoming life. Some souls don't enter until birth or just afterward. To me, this means that there is minimal (if any) damage to a soul during the first trimester, at the very least.

Some souls actually contract for a short womb experience. These tend to be very advanced souls that only need a taste of life in order to complete their life lessons. Sometimes, however, a soul really wants to incarnate and is aborted instead. In these cases, the dispatched soul often incarnates to a different family member or awaits an opportunity to enter through the original pregnant woman, but at a different time.

I once worked with a woman who had four sons. She had become pregnant in college and had aborted the embryo because she and her husband could not take care of a child at that point in their lives. My client, who did not believe in "this stuff," heard the soul of the child during the abortion say "I will return." After graduating, she became pregnant right away. They had the child; my client is sure that it is the same soul that was aborted years before.

We must remember that the Divine plans for all human mishaps, errors, and traumas. We are loved. The soul of the aborted child is loved. We are so much bigger than the events we go through, as are all souls.

## I miscarried. What does this mean?

The body uses miscarriage to release embryos that are physically malformed or genetically unviable. Repetitive miscarriages can be also be caused by these conditions, as well as structural factors such as a tilted uterus. Approximately one in five pregnancies ends in miscarriage,[1] so it is a common experience that doesn't usually require a lot of psychoanalysis. There are times when a miscarriage does involve metaphysical explanations, however.

I worked with a woman who had miscarried three times for no apparent medical reason. I perceived a warring soul trying to get into her womb. This soul, whom my client's soul did not want to give birth to, kept pushing other baby souls out of the way. My client's soul refused to let this violating soul in. Therefore, this violating soul had kept all souls out. We sent a healing to the warring soul. The Divine then took it to heaven, and my client was pregnant with twins within a few months.

### I was adopted. Was this pre-planned?

Many adoptive situations are pre-planned before birth. For one of many reasons, our soul came in through a certain set of parents but needed to be raised by another set of parents.

The various reasons I have seen for pre-planned adoptions are these:

- We needed a specific set of genetics to carry out our destiny.
- We weren't supposed to be adopted but we were anyway.

---

1   www.babycenter.com/0_understanding-miscarriage_252.bc

- We engaged in learning about unconditional love, such as the need to be loved or learn how to love people we aren't technically related to.
- We needed to be raised by people who couldn't get pregnant, and so we came in through a different set of biological parents.

## What are the potential effects of being adopted?

Nearly every adopted person I have worked with has severe abandonment issues. In most cases, an unborn child is bonded with the birth mother via the umbilical bond we discussed earlier. Unless the mother releases this bond and passes it to the adoptive mother, the child will feel an ongoing tug from or push toward the mother. This longing usually transforms into an unmet need and a needy or unfulfilled personality.

Sometimes the biological mother refuses to form an umbilical bond. This obviously subconscious decision can be made with the best of intentions, maybe to spare herself or the baby the sorrow of parting. Having never experienced a bond during its earliest months, however, a child might not know how to bond with anyone else.

I worked with one client who didn't know he was adopted until he was fifty years of age. He only found out when he was searching for his birth certificate in his mother's house and discovered adoption papers instead. He had spent his entire life feeling like he was "missing something." After tracking and then reuniting with his birth parents, this emptiness disappeared.

## I think I was supposed to have a twin. Why would I feel like this?

I have worked often with a "disappearing twin" syndrome. Some statistics assert that one in ten pregnancies is a twin conception, but one of the two or more embryos might disappear because of genetic anomalies or conditions in the womb.

Sometimes this twin was "supposed" to be born but for various reasons, probably physical, could not become a viable embryo. The remaining twin will feel alone, as if his or her best friend is missing. The remaining twin might also be stricken with survivor guilt, an undeserved sense of shame for surviving.

Occasionally, the disappeared twin remains on the scene as a spiritual guide, sometimes becoming a so-called invisible playmate to its sibling. Less frequently, the discarnate twin becomes angry and causes significant disturbance in the surviving twin's life. It wishes that it had been the one born instead.

I worked with a client who could not sleep at night because of a voice. The voice would start at midnight and begin taunting her. It would wrap up the show about 4 AM by calling her a murderer.

I had the image of a pregnant belly and made an educated guess. "When did your mother go into labor?" I asked.

"About midnight," she replied.

And yes, my client was born at about 4 AM.

We performed a regression and discovered she had a twin that had not lived beyond the second trimester. The not-born twin was mad and had been persecuting my client ever since. Once we blessed and released this twin, the voice stopped altogether.

## Why would souls come as twins?

Fraternal twins are two souls that deeply love each other. They usually come to support and inspire each other. Identical twins might be two souls, but just as likely, they are a single soul split in half. In this way, the soul can work on two life lessons or spiritual purposes simultaneously.

We have more twin-plus births occurring currently than ever before, primarily because of fertilization techniques. Potentially, the early bonding between siblings can infuse a greater sense of community within families and, therefore, the world. I believe that this increase in multiple births is also a sign of better things to come on this planet.

## What souls are being born on the planet at this time?

There are more people alive than ever before. This is an exciting time. Souls from all over—different planets, dimensions, and spiritual realms—are journeying here to join a universal movement to help this planet progress.

Souls incarnate in groups, each group undertaking one of the tasks necessary to help us all progress. The soul generations currently represented are as follows:

**Construct souls:** This is the grandparent generation, which holds specific ideas and goals. Often representing strong and traditional values, the members of this group create systems and institutions that establish a secure base for future generations.

**Bridge souls:** Known as the "Baby Boomers," this group bridges the old with the new, seeking to unify spirituality with materiality. As a whole, it has ushered in new ideas, such as those presented by the New Age and quantum physics, while strengthening the foundation of what has come before.

**Indigo souls:** This is the "twenty-something" generation, each member entering with dazzlingly bright ideas. They want freedom, excitement, and something really new. Their ultimate goal is to create higher goals for this world.

**Crystal souls:** These soft and incandescent children are delicate, fragile, and very psychic. They have little karma, meaning that their soul issues are usually healed, but they also lack strong psychic boundaries. They are therefore susceptible to the negativity on this planet, which provides the rest of us a reason to clean up our act.

**Spirit souls:** This is a group of angels sent straight from heaven. They do not need the protection required for crystal souls because they operate from their spiritual essence, not their soul selves. They are here to demonstrate forgiveness and compassion.

# The Spirit World

## Are there ghosts?

Of course.

Only Americans would ask this question, as we are one of the few countries that fails to respect the existence of the invisible. In England, for instance, it is common practice to compare the quality of ghosts in the various bed-and-breakfast establishments. I actually saw a sign in one bed-and-breakfast that stated the following: "Our ghosts serve tea." I cannot say the innkeeper's dead aunt Hazel showed up to serve me tea in the late afternoon, but I was up all night listening to her chatting.

Ghosts are the souls of people who were once alive. For some reason, though, their souls have not yet departed for the "other side." There are many reasons the soul of a deceased person might choose to hang around. Some ghosts do not think they are dead. This ignorance created a problem in my own home when, for months, my son and I were both awakened by midnight giggles and chatter from his room. As if that weren't enough, just when we'd both fallen asleep—for the fourteenth time in an evening—the battery-operated toys would start going at it. "I am Buzz Lightyear" would perforate the silence along with King Kong's roar. When I "checked in" with my clairvoyance, I saw a horde of little boy souls who did not know that they were dead. They sure liked Gabe's toys, though! I requested angels of light to intervene and take the little children to the other side.

Some souls linger to exact revenge or because they are afraid of facing the Divine; they assume they will be sent straight to hell. Other souls remain in order to help their loved ones or to wait for a loved one to die. There are many reasons for their ghostly presence.

Souls have power, even beyond death. One of the strangest circumstances I have encountered involved an older woman who called because every man that had married into her family had died. She had lost three husbands to death; her grandmother had lost one husband, and her mother, two. One of her daughter's husbands had died and her second husband was ill, as was the husband of her recently married second daughter. Through my visioning, I perceived that a haunting was plaguing the men in the family. The storyline that enfolded suggested that a great-grandfather had been in love with a woman who had spurned him; instead, she married the man she loved. He had murdered the husband and forced the woman into marrying him next. He was continuing this pattern energetically. As soon as we released his spirit to the Divine, the ill son-in-laws became well.

### Is there a way to contact a deceased loved one?

The easiest way is to ask the Divine to connect you with the loved one and to pay attention to your intuition.

There are many forms of intuition; you will receive contact via the one or ones that match your personality. Generally, if you are verbal, you will hear messages; if you are visual, you will see messages; is you are physically kinesthetic, you will receive information from nature, your physical surroundings, or through bodily sensations or feelings; and if you are spiritually kinesthetic, you will obtain revelations when praying, meditating, or contemplating, through spirit visitations, or directly from the Divine.

I recommend that you pray to the Divine to arrange connection and then remain open to the unusual. I have one client whose father talks through books, which literally fall off the shelf and open to a specific page. Yet another receives visitations from her deceased child in dreams. Her young son has continued to age in the spirit realm, as if alive, and he fills her in on his activities as a spiritual guide for the living. Know that the passed-over souls have personal journeys, which I discuss in my book *Illuminating the Afterlife*. They might be unavailable to communicate because they are involved on their own evolutionary path.

## What about spiritual guides? Does everyone have one?

Yes; in fact, you have at least two that have been with you since birth. Usually one is an angel or spiritual master and the other is a deceased person. The angel supports our spiritual destiny and the once-alive guide comforts and advises.

As we meander through life, we add different guides, depending on our needs. Off to college? It's sure helpful to be assigned a bookish angel. Going to become a parent? Why not a grandmother or grandfather spirit to coach you?

One of my clients, Bob, was thrilled to learn that his deceased father attended his daughter as a guide. How did he find out? When Katie was three, she started to talk about the "grandpoppa" who was teaching her about "choo-choos." She described a paunchy, bald man wearing overalls. Bob's father had been a train conductor whose physical presence exactly matched Katie's description.

## Are there bad guides?

Just as there are good and bad people, there are good and bad spirits. Many of our problems or misguided efforts at life are caused or reinforced by negative entities.

Some of these are "ancestral hauntings," members of our family lineage that want to continue bossing others around, even when they are dead. They might want revenge. They might not want to be surpassed by the living. They might think they are really helping us. Some negative influences come from past lives. Other demonic forces might be just that, part of the wandering troop of beings that seeks control by manipulating others.

I always tell people to go directly to the Divine for help, requesting that the Divine send guides that are loving and spirit-filled. Don't listen to souls that might appear out of nowhere, even if it's someone you once knew—especially if you didn't like or trust him or her when they were alive. Not every person improves with age, nor does every dead person become wise.

# Across Time and Space

## Does everyone have past lives?

No. Not everyone alive at this time has been incarnate as a human being before.

As discussed in the next section under "Purpose Across Time and Space" (page 169), our planet is at a unprecedented stage. More souls are incarnating than at any other time. Moreover, some spirits are taking on souls in order to incarnate from other planets, galaxies, spiritual realms, and dimensions.

I believe that a spirit—the immortal essence of self— has to slow itself down in order to occupy the material world. I have also noticed that angels, star beings, and other forms of heavenly spirits are paying special attention to this planet at this time. Look at how many people are seeing the immortals! Receiving spiritual guidance! Actually talking about it! If enough humans could only make the swing to goodness, the planet as a whole, including all life forms, guides, and Earth itself, can enter a state of peace. If we can do this, the universe itself can become more of what it is supposed to be: a realm of love.

In my work, I've actually met hundreds of people— usually youngsters—who tell me that they have come here right from the heavens. They don't recall having lived a past life. They know only that they are here to fulfill an important mission: peace.

## What do past lives tell us about our current relationships, purpose, and work?

Most of us return time after time to further our spiritual development. Our spiritual purpose is a goal and a legacy. We must achieve it, one step at a time, ever developing into more of who and what we can be. It's also something we carry with us.

I have a client who is an amazing painter. He recalls several lifetimes of serving as an author and a painter. He spent one lifetime painting the dirt into a famous artist's paintings. His gifts have clearly evolved over time, and his current artistic achievements are magnificent. From dirt—to the skies!

## Did we all come from the same planetary system?

Absolutely not! My friend Wendy and I recently experienced a strange afternoon in a mall, where our lesson emphasized the fact that most of our souls have journeyed to Earth from elsewhere.

We were both walking and talking and suddenly became quiet. I kept seeing people shape-shift, as if they were morphing into alien creatures from the movie about beings from outer space, *Men in Black*. One woman looked like a giant insect; another a huge reptile. Yet another appeared as a troll disguised in human clothes; another was a witch. I admitted to Wendy that I was "feeling strange," and she said the same. We compared stories and discovered that we were both experiencing the same phenomenon. She was able to overhear conversations in the original languages, on top of it. The spell lifted in an hour or so, but we were shaken. (And also amazed that people kept staring at *us*.)

My client base is mainstream. At least 25 percent have admitted to having visions, dreams, memories, and sensations of being from somewhere else. The list I've compiled to date includes the following sites that predated entry into the earth plane:

- Angelic spheres.
- Demonic spheres.
- A variety of stars, including black holes and white holes.
- Other planets, such as the Blue Planet and the thirteenth planet that seemed to have once orbited around our sun.
- Moons and comets.
- Heaven itself or chambers within it.
- Parts of the faery realm or underworld.
- Dimensions that are hard to describe; one client remembered being a dot, yet another hung out as a triangle for a while.
- Elemental states; I remember being the wind for a long time before I ever became a person.

### Do we all enter Earth as an infant?

No. As I implied in the final statement in the last question, some of us have evolved—or devolved—from other places. And many enter the earth realm first through a nonhuman form. I once worked with a child who asked if he could go back to being a rock.

Still others of us took more or less direct routes. Since I was a small child, I have had recall of my first time on Earth. I was actually an angel—a Shining One, in fact. Stories are still told about the Shining Ones who walk this planet at Midsummer in the northern countries, sharing truth and granting wishes. The Divine told me that he/she needed me to incarnate but I had to retain full consciousness in order to fulfill my mission. I asked how I was to do this, and the Divine pointed out the body of a four-year-old Hebrew girl.

Her soul had just left for the heavens as her father had been beating her. The Divine told me that if I entered her body, I would retain clear memory of my true self but would also have to work through the little girl's human trauma and karma, especially her victim issues. I agreed and still remember the claustrophobic feeling of being dropped into this small, cold body.

A few years ago, the Divine told me that I could leave this planet—I had completed the task of wrapping up the girl's karma, or lessons, and didn't need to suffer anymore. (It only took two thousand years.) I decided to stay, and my life has improved since. I believe I *had* to accept earth lessons in order to gain the compassion and understanding necessary to fulfill my own true destiny.

## Tell a little about Atlantis and Lemuria and why they figure into past-life work.

I have traveled around the world and often find myself researching esoteric materials in some of the strangest places, including libraries in England, Wales, Arizona, Greece, Scotland, Belize, and Morocco—as well as inside the annals of my own intuition.

My sense of earth history incorporates the so-called mythologies (or realities) of Atlantis and Lemuria. I believe it's important to at least consider the idea that these people existed, as the themes involved explain so much of current reality and the problems we're facing as a people today.

I'll reveal my tale in story form.

Once upon a time, there were three planets in the Pleiadian star system. Beings from other planetary systems occupied two of these planets; the other was uninhabitable.

Excelling in intuition and science, the inhabitants of these planets determined that both planets would explode in a few eons. They moved to the planet that would be inhabitable for the longest time period and began to explore different galaxies for a mass migration. They found Earth.

The first wave of settlers left for Earth and settled amongst the primitive people already inhabiting the planet. They lived peacefully among them, teaching basic survival skills and ways of love. They built pyramids and megalithic structures in order to continue contact with their Pleiades brethren and in general lived in oneness with all. Their job was to prepare the way for the second surge of settlers from the Pleiades. Thus they dwelled in simplicity for several thousand years, surviving deluges, famines, and other natural catastrophes. I believe the stories of these people are encoded in the sacred texts of the Hawaiian kahunas, the Shipibo Indians of the Peruvian Amazon, the Cherokee Tsalgi, the Kung! in the Kalahari, and other indigenous populations I've walked amongst. We would call these the Lemurians.

Meanwhile, the Pleiades fellowship continued to progress, but more technologically. They employed crystals and other devices for healing, information storage, and energy. A power elite emerged that used this technology to master the less influential. When it came time to transfer to Earth, the dominators decided to move their members, technological gear, and instruments first, even if it meant leaving much of the population behind. This is what they did.

I have a past-life memory of being one of the elite who decided to save as many people as possible. As a child, I recalled being splayed in a wormhole, or stargate, holding it open until at least some of the left behind could move through. I still remember that there was one small girl who had to depart. I held the portal open, even though it meant that I was crushed within it. The people who arrived on Earth during this exodus could be called the Atlanteans.

The Atlanteans continued their ways on planet Earth until their experimentation led to a final deluge and breakdown of the natural order. This culminated in an ice age, and humanity had to start over.

Our major cultural themes are rooted in these stories: devotion to the natural and goodness versus the manipulation of power and technology; advancement of the whole versus the greed of the few. Even the Superman story, which features an infant sent to Earth when his planet is destroyed, is encompassed in this age-old tale. Whether I have recorded our human history accurately or not, I'm one of many who believe that Earth is seeded from other places. We brought our problems with us. Perhaps it's time to solve them.

## How does the story of Adam and Eve figure in to your ideas?

Let me tell you my theory. I believe that God created this planet and other physical planets and set angels to watch over us. Some of these angels were jealous of humanity. We had souls; angels "only" have spirits. These envious angels mated with women, the original "Eves," to create progeny with souls. (This story is actually biblical and found in Genesis.) This sexual mixup is equivalent to eating of the Tree of Knowledge of Good and Evil.

But we weren't ready. Along with the rebellious angels, we became stuck in the lower energetic form, thinking we now had to re-achieve heaven. But guess what? The original creation continued alongside our fallen one. It is attended by the non-fallen angels, such as Michael and Gabriel, but also our own spirits. I think many of the guides we see are ourselves—the higher selves we talk to are actually us, guiding ourselves into an awakening. In fact, this world is really but a shadow, an alternative, parallel universe; the "other" realm is the real one. We've only to recognize that *we* are the higher self, the angel lighting the way for others.

# Relationship Questions

## Why do I have immediate reactions to some people?

This is a common occurrence that usually indicates one of three situations.

First, you knew this person in a past life. Do you think you will forget the thief that stole all your cows that time? Or that great kisser?

Second, you pre-planned the meeting. Your two souls might have contracted before birth—or even, just moments ago, in the ethers—to meet at a specific time. I was once awakened from a deep sleep and told by my guide to go the convenience store. My kids were not home, so I went. There was a young mother looking woe-begone, holding the hands of a little girl. I felt immediate and great warmth for them. The woman's husband had deserted them, and I was able to give them a ride to her own mother's house. I believe that I was supposed to help her at that time. Perhaps the woman and child were dear friends in a past life? Alternatively, maybe we met in a dream the night before? I don't know.

Third, this person's pattern might remind us of some-one else's. Every spirit has its own personal blueprint, but there are similarities between those of the same soul group. You might recognize a friend's imprint, for instance, in that of a stranger's.

## Are people naturally heterosexual or homosexual?

Certain souls are more male than female, as defined by stereotypical and human characteristics. Some souls are simply more feminine in that they are intuitive, warm, loving, and receptive. Others are more masculine in that they are linear, dominating, active, and giving. These individualized souls often incarnate in a like-minded body, but not always. Sometimes a male soul enters a feminine body and vice versa. Sometimes these individuals appear more masculine or feminine than others of their gender or become homosexual because of this.

Souls often choose their sexual orientation before birth, usually because the choice is necessary for their destiny plan. A soul would then select the genes that predispose it toward that orientation.

Once in a while, the plan goes awry. I have a client who was born a woman but always knew he was supposed to have landed in a male body. As a child, he told this to his parents, who accepted his analysis without question. He later went through a sex-change operation with the full support of his parents.

Sometimes abuse convinces someone to go against his or her organic nature. I offer another story, however, to provide balance. I once worked with a married male client who spent two years working with a Christian counselor to try and "purge" himself of his homosexuality. At the end of these two years, the counselor looked at my client and said, "You're right. You are gay. The Bible has to be wrong."

## Do animals have souls?

Most animals do have souls. They are also connected through their species to an animal spirit, a greater spirit that links their individual souls to each other. Just as humans incarnate for a specific purpose, so do most animals (and reptiles, fish, and birds).

When people ask about animals, they are usually curious about their own companion animals: dogs, cats, horses, even rabbits. Each of these makes their way to your home and heart, where they instruct, guide, and learn. My dog Honey is Gabe's best friend and eases Gabe's heart when he is sad. Coco is a blind, deaf dog, wise beyond her years. We call her the shaman dog because she performs healing. Max the guinea pig is the disciplinarian. He stands up and points his paws when someone isn't being nice. Johnny Cat is just plain smart; his purpose is to show the rest of us how to use our brains. Then there's Wilma the Turtle. I'm not sure what her purpose is, but she knows.

## Can you see the future of a relationship?

We have free will; it's not my job to intrude. I worked with one woman who visited with me a dozen times. She was married, with no children. Every image I received showed that her marriage would dissolve, but my inner sense was to keep quiet. Finally, she and her husband divorced. She asked me why I hadn't said anything to her about this. Truthfully, I said the information would affect her free will, and that the decision wasn't mine, it was hers.

Sometimes I am compelled to say something. For a male client, I received clear images of a divorce. In the first scene, I envisioned a ring on his finger; in the second, there was no ring. I then saw a vision in which he packed his bags and moved into a hotel; I could feel the pain of betrayal in his heart. Instead of sharing all these images, I asked the Divine what I was supposed to say. I was told to tell him to watch what happened in his house the next time he was out of town. I did, suggesting that he might want to return home early. He did and discovered his wife in bed with one of her many lovers. He moved out immediately.

## What is it like to date a clairvoyant?

I am not sure, since I'm the clairvoyant! I do not use my gifts to pry into someone's secrets or their minds, but my intuition does inform me about certain issues. With one man I dated, I had a sense that he was not telling me the truth. I did not ask to see pictures or to have the Divine send me information. Rather, the sense grew until one day, I suddenly knew what had happened. He had lied by telling me that he was going somewhere to take care of his children when instead, he re-engaged with an ex-wife. I was upset, but I knew that the Divine wanted me to know the truth so I made choices with my eyes open, not closed. I am sure each of us has senses like this that warn when things are not quite what they appear to be.

I HAVE LEARNED that if one advances confidently
in the direction of his dreams, and endeavors to
live the life he has imagined, he will meet with
a success unexpected in common hours.

—Henry David Thoreau

# Q&A:
## *Work*

Work invites us to share our spiritual gifts with the world. It allows us to succeed at our spiritual purpose or mission, which always involves creating more love on this planet. Each of us gives and receives love in a unique way. Work is one of the most important avenues for creating, sharing, and receiving our special form of love.

Work is not a career label. It is not constricted to the employment description we provide to the Internal Revenue Service. It is not labor or toil or only what earns money.

Our spiritual work can and does, however, involve fulfilling duties and responsibilities. It might involve being paid; it certainly includes feeling gratified. Real work, however—the work that we are here on this planet to do—must accomplish a fundamental and singular goal: true work enlightens. True work pulls forth the light that we are and radiates it into the world.

In this section, we explore the many questions I am often asked about true work: our spiritual mission, or calling; our spiritual path; our destiny and vocation. I present this information in several sections: True Work as Spiritual Purpose, Purpose Across Time and Space, Spiritual Gifts, Work and Money, Blocks and Challenges, Spiritual World and Work, Work and the World Around Us, and Determining Your Purpose. As you read these questions and answers, let your own queries come to the surface. Answer them with your own intuition. We are all equipped with the faculties necessary to hear, see, and sense who we are—and where we are going.

# True Work as Spiritual Purpose

## What is true work?

True work is the active part of love.

We are here to love. We are here to learn about love, feel love, accept love, and *love*. Relationships tend to circulate love between the people involved. Work takes the lessons we learn in relationship and expands them into the greater world.

## What does true work have to do with having a "spiritual calling" or "spiritual purpose"?

Various spiritualities have different names for true work. Well-known terms include purpose, mission, vocation, calling, and destiny. Fulfilling your spiritual mission is also synonymous with phrases including "being on the path" and "following your calling." These words point to the meaning of true work, which is to express one's essence and spiritual gifts in order to create more love.

## Where did my spiritual purpose originally come from?

This is a very important question. In order to live our spiritual purpose and achieve our destiny, we have to understand why we even have one.

The short answer is this: we spin our purpose and dreams in cooperation with the Divine.

The longer answer is a story.

Once upon a time, a long time ago, we were all united within the greater All. Whatever "God" is, we know that God is love. God is the Divine, the Great Spirit, the Holy Power, the Goddess, the Buddha, the Creator, the All-Good. God is what God is.

In this union with the All, we were what we really are. In this space of unity, we could be our true selves: spirits, eternal and infinite beings formed in the image of the Divine.

As spirits, we had incredible powers. We were invincible, lovable, and all-loving. A spirit can no more be injured than air can be cut with a sharp knife. Made of love, our spirits knew themselves to be deserving of love. Our spirits participated in perfection.

Not everything was perfect. The nature of love is to create more love. The Divine was not content to float alone in the universe. Why would each of us be satisfied with a relatively static state? Each of us yearned to make a difference. We longed to fulfill a higher purpose. We pledged to leave heaven and create more love elsewhere. We decided to venture into the void, where love did not yet exist—nor anything else.

The Divine assigned to each of us a spiritual truth or set of truths to integrate into physical matter. This, then, is our work, this sharing of truth in order to create more heaven on earth. To accomplish this goal, the union of spirits formulated a way each of us could achieve our destiny, an individual plan. We are still conducting this destiny in a process that many call "following our spiritual path."

Our spiritual purpose, or true work, is to actualize the divine truths that we have been assigned through everything we say, do, or think. As we imprint the world with these truths, we join with others doing the same. Together, we are manifesting a greater reality than one ever known before. Our tears, sweat, and pain go into the process, as do our inherent perfection and loving nature. Together, we are creating a world—a universe—that will be even better than the one experienced within the divine womb, for it will be empowered by experience and infused with hard-won wisdom.

### You say that my spirit's work is to imprint spiritual truths in the world. How are these carried into the physical reality?

Your spirit is essentially perfect; it cannot be damaged. It embraces and understands only love. In order to share the divine truths it carries, however, your spirit needed to be able to feel these truths. It needed to be changed by them. It needed to gain experience. To do so, it had to be willing to be wounded.

How can you become something you aren't? Because our spirit could not change its basic nature, it added to it. Our spirit created a second self, one that could be injured in the course of duty—one that could learn, grow, touch, feel, succeed, and fail. It formed a soul.

Unlike our timeless spirit, our soul can modify itself for every incarnation and experience. Unlike our spirit, our soul can imagine away love, to the point of believing itself unlovable, worthless, and bad. Unlike our spirit, our soul can become fragmented and damaged. But unlike our spirit, our soul can also transform—and not only due to loving interactions. The soul can also learn from unloving experiences.

Our soul's main vehicle for expressing its work is to occupy a body. Our bodies carry our spiritual truths and enable us to transfer the energy of these truths into physical reality. Through our bodies, we touch reality—and are touched in return. We share all we have learned—and learn more about love with each learning.

## Is my spiritual purpose limited to work as defined by our culture?

Absolutely not. This is why I emphasize spiritual terms for true work, such as calling, mission, and destiny, rather than the more culturally accepted labels, which include career, profession, job, employment, and occupation.

Our spiritual work might include a career or job. Because we are essentially spirits interacting through our souls via a body, however, everything we do constitutes work. This includes buying groceries, going to the library, or renewing your motor vehicle permit. It involves how you maintain your domicile, be it a studio apartment or a large mansion. Your spiritual work includes any and all interactions with this planet and your fellow beings on this planet.

My work, for instance, involves embodying the truths of love, healing, and happiness. Would I be expressing love if I spent all my time working with clients, to the exclusion of talking with friends and taking care of my children? Would I be teaching happiness to my children if we only interacted through homework and the dictates of household chores? Absolutely not. Our true work encompasses all aspects of our life. It is a matter of being or living on the path, not just punching a time clock.

## What does the phrase "being" or "living on the path" mean?

Being on the path means that we are expressing our spirit, or essence, through everything that we do and are. It also means that we are ever evolving—that we are constantly learning about the spiritual truths of others and ourselves.

## How do I know if I am on the path or not?

Begin by assuming that you are on the path. The real issue is whether you have to negotiate a few more turns on the path before you are expressing all of who you are.

## What are the indicators of being on the path?

True work—your spiritual calling—encompasses all of your major life experiences, including those you believe to be minor, as well as those that have been traumatic. In fact, the single most important indicator of being on the path, or fulfilling our destiny, is that we have gathered the entirety of our past, analyzed it for its gifts, and can now use everything we have experienced to help others.

## Can you explain how work makes use of everything we have ever experienced?

I am going to use my own life as an example to help provide an explanation for this question.

I spent years in corporate America, where I taught business ethics and served as a public relations professional. After that, I worked in fundraising for a large nonprofit organization. I never would have guessed that these experiences would have meant anything given the direction I chose next.

During this same time, I was also exploring the worlds of healing and intuition. I took one of the first classes in therapeutic touch (hands-on healing) offered in Minneapolis. I also had the opportunity to travel to unusual places, meeting diviners, healers, shamans, and mystics. I encountered a mountain with witches in Venezuela and learned how they told fortunes; I met a local healer in Japan who touched my then-pregnant belly and told me how to care for my son; and I studied plant medicine with healers in Belize, Costa Rica, Mexico, Hawaii, and Peru. I had no idea what all this meant. But the Divine informed me to quit my job and begin a healing business.

I like planning, and rather than just take the Divine at its word, I started a marketing communication business. I also made some pink business cards created at my local

copy shop that gave my job title as "Psychic." I was morti-
fied at the thought of passing them out and was just about
to hide them in my purse when another copy shop customer spotted the word *psychic* on the card and grabbed a
few, telling me she'd send me clients. That was the beginning—I was in business. Not the business I *thought* I was
starting, the business the Divine had in mind for me.

The marketing communication company did not succeed, and I slowly began running my intuition business. I
was too business-oriented to let my intuition business fail,
but I felt torn in half. What had happened to the "first"
me—the businesswoman who knew her way around a
corporate boardroom? The one who had majored in English and philosophy? Who was this pink lady who made
her living talking to invisible beings?

It took years for me to feel completely "on-purpose."
That occurred only when the various parts of me and
my background began integrating. I began teaching intuitive communication to corporate people. I perceived the
many connections between mothering and consulting.
My daily intuitive healing business touched on themes I
had addressed my entire adult life, from therapy to parenting to cleaning the house. My spiritual background
suddenly solidified, and I linked the seeming opposites of
spirituality and religion.

One day, I woke up and realized that I was on-purpose.
My life made sense, every component. I was even making
use of my English major by writing books. That day was

a sign. It uplifted and compelled me to continue to grow and stretch. I now understood that there are no wasted events, simply people who waste their life learning without becoming.

## How can tragic events compose a part of my purpose?

Repeatedly, I have seen that destiny emerges from the life that has been led to this point in time. While the influences of positive experiences are always easy to spot, negative experiences have a surprisingly constructive effect. It has been said that fate is what we are handed, and destiny is what we do with it. We are not here to go through some memorized patterns. We are here to learn and think and love.

One example of how the bad and the good experiences weave a whole cloth is a client who became a paraplegic in a car accident. She was in her early twenties at this time, and for ten years, she thought her life was over. She had been an Olympic-quality long-distance runner, and prior to the accident had decided to become a coach. Following the accident, her sense of purpose was destroyed.

When we began to work together, she was suicidal. We had met for a few sessions before I asked a question that helped her break through. I received a picture of God, dressed as a female high-school teacher, standing before my client, forcing her to take a pen and begin to write an essay: "What have you learned by being a paraplegic that you would want to share with others?" Once written, the essay was distributed to others in the classroom.

My client smiled and talked for almost an hour. Now I smiled and pointed out that she had just introduced herself to her true calling, a way of living that shares something vital and unique about oneself with others. Within a few years, she had authored a book and started a business coaching children and adults with physical challenges. But her specialty was emotional and mental well-being as well as physical challenges. My client's purpose made use of *all* her life experiences—the positive ones and the seemingly negative ones as well.

## What might be an example of a truly satisfying purpose?

I once asked this question of Don Augustine, a shaman with whom I studied in the Peruvian Amazon.

I had spent several weeks learning about sacred ceremony and plant medicine from this shaman, who was originally trained as a Catholic priest. At one point, I asked him what he thought his purpose was as a healer.

Before answering, Don Augustine explained about the people in his jungle community, a small village called Yushintita, about two hours by motorboat, six hours by slow boat, down the Amazon from Iquitos, Peru. The girls usually marry their boyfriends when they are both around age thirteen, after which the two have several children. As it's a Catholic country, women and children don't generally use birth control, so the babies keep coming. When it becomes impossible to care financially for the children, the boy or young man turns to alcohol and deserts the family, at which point the mother and children are left to negotiate the world alone.

Don Augustine considered that it was his calling to help the girls and the boys to make better choices. This was his simple phrase to explain everything he did. Don Augustine performed healing for all who came to him. He then used his funds to buy computers for the children and sponsor birth control for the girls and women. He worked with outside visitors to provide desks for the schoolrooms and influence education. For those young people who fell into the patterns of their parents, he offered psychological insight and healing, drawing upon the spirit of Nature to assist his work. In short, he helped young people to make better choices and older folks to heal from the poor choices they had made.

Don Augustine's simple responses point to the nature of true work. Exemplary work is not complicated. It draws upon tradition but often expands outside of the box of the status quo. It fills the cracks of someone's life and even then seeps around it, overflowing to assist others. It addresses contemporary concerns. It helps people makes life-enhancing choices. It employs compassion for those with problems. It holds self and others to a loving standard. In summation, true work makes full use of our spiritual gifts.

# Purpose Across Time and Space

## What do past lives have to do with my current spiritual purpose?

Your spirit develops through your soul lifetime after lifetime. If your overriding spiritual purpose is to share love, for instance, your soul might facilitate this goal as a mother in one lifetime and a train conductor in another. Each set of experiences builds upon the last and leads to a greater expression of destiny.

## For what purpose are so many of us on this planet right now?

This planet is in a change point—a crossroads. We either embrace the teaching of truth, the truth of love, or regress.

Many spiritual groups suggest that this is the fourth or fifth age on this planet—that, in fact, we've been devolving. At every epoch, we have made the wrong choice and have degraded ourselves further into cruelty and prejudice.

We don't have much further to go to, unfortunately—or maybe fortunately, for now is the time to decide if we're willing to accept the power of individual choice and do what's right, no matter what. If enough people can do this, we might not only make it as a race but elevate our entire world to a higher place—one of love.

## Where have all these souls come from?

There are more souls incarnate right now than ever before. They come from all over—as do we.

Where is "all over"? Other planets, dimensions, parallel or concurrent realities, galaxies, angelic realms, past-life time periods—perhaps even future times. Some souls have been here before and others have not. This is a great gathering. As small and tiny a planet as this is, it is one of the "choice points" in the multiverse. What we decide here, for good and bad, ripples throughout all time and space and steers other spirits and souls to choose love—or not.

# Spiritual Gifts:
*Tools of Truth to Carry Out Your Mission*

## What are spiritual gifts, and what do they have to do with my true work?

Our spiritual purpose, or destiny—our true work—is to integrate spiritual truths into the world. Spiritual truths are ethereal; they cannot be seen or touched. We only perceive the presence of a truth if it is being articulated through action.

When a spirit inhabits a body, spiritual truths are demonstrated as spiritual gifts. These abilities allow us to create more love on this planet.

## What do the spiritual gifts do?

A spiritual gift serves others. Most religions and spiritual texts emphasize the importance of knowing and sharing our spiritual gifts with others; that is because they are the key to achieving our destiny and living our spiritual calling.

A famous source that describes spiritual gifts is the Christian New Testament. Here, the apostle Paul asserts that we all have spiritual gifts, such as healing, manifesting, encouraging, caring, prophesying, and dream analysis. Nearly every indigenous culture also speaks of the same set of abilities. In the Hindu tradition, the ultimate gifts are called the *siddhi*.

From a clairvoyant's point of view, spiritual gifts evolve through a long and sometimes arduous process, one that begins deep inside the energetic body. Once activated, these gifts allow us to achieve our spiritual destiny, or true work, through helping others.

## How do the spiritual gifts evolve?

When our soul enters a body, it encodes its spiritual truths into the chakras, energy bodies that transform fast-moving psychic energy into slow-moving sensory energy, and vice versa. We have twelve major chakras, and each of these serves as the source of a spiritual truth.

Initially, these gifts operate psychically. This fundamental use of the gifts assures the individual's survival. With training, these innate gifts become intuitive abilities, aptitudes for dealing with psychic and sensory information. When we decide to use our gifts and the truths they represent for divine purposes, these gifts transform into full spiritual gifts, extraordinarily strong powers for good.

## What are the different spiritual gifts?

The chart on the opposite page is a synopsis of these gifts in relation to the chakras, which are each located in a different part of the body.

| Chakra | Location | Spiritual gift/s |
|--------|----------|------------------|
| First | Hip | Manifesting |
| Second | Abdomen | Creativity, compassion |
| Third | Solar plexus | Administration, mental acuity |
| Fourth | Heart | Love, healing |
| Fifth | Throat | Communication, sharing words of knowledge |
| Sixth | Forehead | Vision |
| Seventh | Top of head | Spirituality |
| Eighth | 2 inches above head | Shamanism |
| Ninth | Arm's length above head | Idealism, harmonizing |
| Tenth | 1½ feet underground | Naturalism, environmental sensitivity, historian |
| Eleventh | Film around body, hands, and feet | Command of natural and supernatural powers |
| Twelfth | Clear bubble around entirety of body | Mastery (of individual destiny) |

### Does everyone have the same gifts?

No. Just as we are all unique spirits and carry individual-ized spiritual truths, so do we have different gifts. Our gifts operate through the chakras, however, and we all have the same chakra system. This means that we have a lot in common with people who draw upon the same chakras. For instance, singers use the gift of communication, available through the fifth chakra, and painters call upon the sixth-chakra ability of visioning.

### Why don't I feel like my gifts are special?

Look around you. The human race is competitive. We compete to own the best real estate, to make—and spend—the most money. We even want to look younger than we looked when we were teenagers. We have to remember the following:

- Each person is unique and has a completely exclusive purpose.

- In order for the world to become the heaven it can be, *every living being* must express his or her purpose.

- Someone else cannot compete with you, or you with them. Only you can accomplish what you came here to accomplish.

### What makes my use of my spiritual gifts so unique?

We all have a unique spiritual mission, and even people who access the very same spiritual gifts will use them in different ways and for individualized reasons. In addition, people mix gifts. For instance, some will draw upon five gifts to accomplish their goals, and others might use only one or two.

I work with two people who are each professional singers. We established earlier that singing requires the use of the fifth chakra, which is located in the throat. Both of these individuals therefore use the spiritual gift of communication in order to express their spiritual purpose.

One woman, however, is an opera singer who performs in international venues dedicated to achieving world peace. She is therefore also tapping into the ninth chakra and the spiritual gifts of harmonizing. Her ultimate purpose is to use both gifts to promote peace.

The other client is a rock-and-roll star. She is as accomplished in dancing gyration-style as she is in belting out music. In addition to accessing her fifth chakra, the rock star also utilizes her first chakra when dancing and the sixth-chakra ability for designing a visual forum. Her summative purpose might read something like this: *To stimulate power and passion in others through a medley of creative expressions.*

While both women are singers, they apply their gifts in very different ways and for different results.

## How are the spiritual gifts activated?

Our gifts are intact when we are born, but we do not usually need to access them fully until we are adults. This

means that, in general, our gifts lie dormant until we are
ready to offer them to the world.

They activate or fully open for different reasons. There
are ideal conditions—and less than ideal situations, as well.
These include the following:

> **Age development:** At a certain age, each chakra
> is programmed to mature. The first chakra,
> for instance, is awakened when we are in the
> womb until we are six months of age. The
> chakra of physicality and manifesting, it adjusts
> to related issues in the environment. If our
> parents are scared about money, for instance, we
> will probably dampen our manifesting abilities.
> If our parents are open to prosperity, our own
> manifesting aptitudes will be heightened. (See
> page 178's chart on age development and the
> activation of the gifts.)

> **Pre-birth decisions:** We create our soul plan before
> birth in a region called the white zone. The
> purpose of this plan is to formulate a destiny
> path. At this point, we decide when some of
> our gifts will open and under what conditions.
> For instance, we might select people to meet,
> educational opportunities, and job offers that
> could assist us with our purpose. If these events
> happen, we will be "on the path" and able to
> apply our spiritual gifts when we need to. No
> matter what we think is going to happen, life

has a way of throwing us interesting detours. We
might not follow our plan perfectly or might
be thrown off by another's inability to follow
through on his or her soul commitments. This
means that certain gifts might not open on
time—or not even open at all.

**Accidental occurrences:** The world is chaotic. This
serves and hurts us. Perhaps life did not unfold
as we had planned, and we never developed an
ability to be compassionate. Maybe Dad married
the wrong woman, and we never felt loved.
Because of this, we have failed to share love with
our spouse or children, and we don't get along
with our coworkers. We might now be "off-
purpose," or unable to fulfill our destiny. The
original problem was not our fault. We might
even know there is a missing ingredient in our
grab bag of gifts. Nonetheless, we'll be unable
to complete our destined plan and will probably
feel a sense of loss.

**Divine intervention:** What if life hasn't gone as
spiritually planned? We are all guided. There is
still hope—and divine intervention.

# Age Development and the Activation of the Gifts

Chakras are frequency based. The colors listed after each chakra describe its particular vibration, or frequency. This information assists a clairvoyant with psychically perceiving someone's gifts and abilities. For instance, someone with a lot of red in his or her energy system will be a potential manifester.

Regarding chakra development, after age fifty-six, the chakras usually begin to recycle in seven-year blocks. For instance, between fifty-six and sixty-three years, someone renews his or her first chakra and manifestation gifts.

| Chakra/Color | Age of Activation |
|---|---|
| First/red | Womb to 6 months |
| Second/orange | 6 months to 2½ years |
| Third/yellow | 2½ to 4½ years |
| Fourth/green | 4½ to 6½ years |
| Fifth/blue | 6½ to 8½ years |
| Sixth/purple | 8½ to 14 years |
| Seventh/white | 14 to 21 years |
| Eighth/black | 21 to 28 years |
| Nine/gold | 28 to 35 years; also preconception |
| Ten/brown | 35 to 42 years; also preconception |
| Eleven/rose | 42 to 49 years |
| Twelve/clear | 49 to 56 years |

| Explanation of Ability |
| :---: |
| Manifesting develops our physical self and ability to secure basic needs |
| Creativity opens our ability to express and compassion soothes others' emotional needs |
| Processing and organizing intuitive and provable data |
| Regulating relationships and directing universal healing energy |
| Receiving and communicating intuitive and audible guidance; musical and teaching capabilities |
| Providing inspirational vision and strategic thinking |
| Connecting with spirituality and spirit world, prophetic knowing |
| Accessing past-life abilities and shamanic powers |
| Opening to individual soul purpose and global understandings; harmonizing self with world; selecting genes and energetics to fulfill our soul purpose |
| Connecting self with natural world; providing environmental sensitivity; emphasizing historical matters; programming genes to fulfill destiny |
| Enabling command of natural and supernatural forces; leadership |
| Personal mastery |

## If the gifts are most open in adulthood, why are some children so gifted?

Some individuals create soul or life plans that call for an early activation of certain gifts. Examples include musical prodigies like Bach and Mozart, and modern musicians like Yo-Yo Ma. Many contemporary sport stars excelled in their sport when they were young. In order to be on-purpose and help the world, these youngsters needed access to their abilities early in their lives. This does not mean, however, that their lives will be restricted to this particular gift.

## When working with clients, how do you know which spiritual gifts they have?

As a clairvoyant, I perceive the spiritual gifts as colors emanating from the chakras. People with a lot of red energy, for instance, have strong first chakras and therefore the gift of manifesting. People with a lot of gold color have an active ninth chakra and are called to help the global community.

## How can I determine my own gifts?

There are many ways to determine your gifts. My book *Attracting Prosperity Through the Chakras* provides a quiz and full outline of the various gifts. Here are a few other ideas:

> **Visit the past:** What skills and interests did you exhibit as a child? We are often most willing to be ourselves at young ages.

**Look for trouble:** What were you most frequently punished for while growing up? Chances are, your parents might have tried to shut you down in the areas the Divine wanted you to open up.

**Ask for dreams:** When sleeping, our soul is free to connect with our guides and the Divine. Ask for dreams to clarify your abilities and purpose.

**Ask your friends:** Sometimes our friends know us better than we know ourselves. Develop a list of questions and take a poll. What do they think you should be doing with your life? At what do you excel? What kind of people can you help?

**Color your world:** Using the information in this book about chakras and their colors, check out your wardrobe. Examine your environment. What colors stand out? How do they make you feel? Your highest gifts might correlate to your favorite colors.

**Regress—the right way:** Work with a trained shaman or therapist to review your past—and maybe your soul plan—to see why you came into this lifetime. What are you here to accomplish?

**Use the system:** Try taking an aptitude test. There are many solid personality reviews that can help you evaluate who you really are.

# Work and Money

## What is the relationship between work and money?

Most people equate work with money. The thinking goes like this: the more "on-purpose" you are, the more money you will make. The more money you make, the more valuable you are as a person.

If true work is about our spiritual calling, then it has nothing to do with money—at one level. Children, friends, and other loved ones are priceless; how can we put a value on the relationship part of our purpose? How much should a healer charge for healing cancer? Money cannot quantify our value.

Money is a cultural recognition of value, not a spiritual one. Having said that, our ability to accept a reward for services delivered indicates our willingness to be both practical and self-valuing. Because of this, I often coach clients to charge a just fee for their work.

A brilliant therapist once had a hard time charging a fair fee for his work. Under his care, most of his patients felt better about themselves, but he felt guilty taking money from his patients—despite the fact that most were wealthy. He simply undercharged. In a session, he and I performed a regression and returned to a past life in which he had been a priest.

The church was pressuring him to sell prayers to his congregation. Against his better judgment, he acquiesced. Those without money did not receive any prayers and were sure that the lack of blessing equated to a condemnation to hell. My client felt so guilty about being part of this greedy manipulation that he decided he would never "cheat" anyone again. He subsequently decided, on a soul level, that charging anything for his time "hurt" people.

The problem was that he had learned the wrong lesson; he had not forgiven himself. Worse, he was also carrying the guilt and shame of the entire Catholic Church.

When I pointed out that he was paying for more than his own bad behavior, the therapist looked at me, startled. If we own more issues than are ours to deal with, we are preventing others from learning their lessons too.

In summary, someone who is on-purpose will value his or her time, as well as another's.

## Is it ethical to "not work" at a paying job?

People who don't work are often accused of being lazy or off-purpose. Some people are employed but not on the path. And some people are unemployed and living fully purposeful lives.

The key to answering this question is to look at the issue of motivation. Some people are unethically unemployed, meaning they would be better people—and better able to help others—if they worked. Insufficient and unethical reasons for unemployment include the following:

- Escape hard work
- Live off the welfare system
- Fear of failure
- Immaturity
- Arrogance

For instance, I worked with a mother of six children who had never had a full-time job. Now, normally, I would say she worked harder on a daily basis than many people employed in jobs outside of the home, except that she had spent twenty-five years avoiding responsibility. Although she had lost a child, she had never cried. Although her husband attempted to communicate with her, in all those years, she only acted happy to see him once. Although she took care of her children's physical needs, she had never hugged them. Four of her six children were medicated for being "too emotional." If this mother's real purpose involved being a mother, she was delinquent. It was obvious to me that she was hiding behind motherhood rather than expressing her spirit through it. The issue was not that she didn't make any money, it was that she was avoiding her destiny.

Some people hide behind their money. I worked with an Austrian woman who was extraordinarily rich. She entered my office on a waft of perfume and immediately began complaining about everyone she knew. Her son did not see her often enough. Her daughter-in-law did not know how to cook. Her friends did not wear the right clothes. Within minutes, my head was reeling. The room was so full of her negativity that it was hard for me to open to divine guidance.

Concentrating hard, I asked the Divine for an image and received only one picture—another one of those pictures that I hate to present. Taking a deep breath, I told her what I saw.

"All I can see is a big bag of money. You are holding it by the top and keep hitting others with it." Accompanying this picture was a message, which I then delivered. "Just having money doesn't give you an excuse to be selfish. You need to start giving of yourself, not just taking from others."

She flew out of my office in a huff. This was another case of concentrating on others' faults and therefore avoiding destiny.

### Are there good reasons to work without pay?

There are some very good reasons—ones that are truly spirit-filled—to not work at a regular paying job. They include the following:

- Our gifts are better used in volunteer or unpaid capacities, when we can afford these positions.

- We are called to parenting and can afford to do this full-time.

- We are ill or otherwise challenged and cannot work; however, we still help others when called to do so.

- We are retired and can now be of service in a different way than before.
- We are in mission work and are not directly paid for our expertise.
- We are too young to work and need to be cared for.
- We are in an emotional or spiritual crisis.
- We are able to deliver love through some other non-paying service, such as babysitting for our grandchildren for no salary.

The most important criterion for not having a job is this: if we are supported and can be fiscally responsible, we are of a mature age, and someone else isn't sacrificing for us.

I worked with a woman who was devoted to mission work through her synagogue. She had spent the entire twenty years of her marriage volunteering for youth and elderly programs, in addition to aiding her own sick mother and the mother of her husband. Her husband financially supported her through all her charitable work, but he was exhausted.

For over a decade, he had been asking her to get a job. He was tired of his profession, worn out, and yearned to have a partner share the financial load. My client thought it was her right to stay at home and was surprised when her husband asked for a divorce. He said he just couldn't take it anymore.

My client asked me why God had allowed this to happen. Wasn't she a saintly woman? Hadn't she been fulfilling her spiritual destiny? When I told her that purpose includes being responsible for both self and others, she grew angry.

"Are you implying I wasn't a good wife?" she asked.

As a response, I saw a picture of the cartoon Calvin from the strip *Calvin and Hobbes*, where Calvin is wringing the neck of his tiger friend, Hobbes, while muttering, "I can do anything I want. You're only alive if you serve my purpose."

The message to my client was that in her quest for spiritual fulfillment, she had been wringing the lifeblood of her husband. How on-purpose had she really been?

## How do you manifest or make money when you are on-purpose?

A dream helped me to personally define my purpose and understand how to manifest through my purpose. I went to sleep one night, asking how I would make money while living on the path. I had read all the books that say "do what you love and the money will follow," but I had also seen a lot of people feeling good about their work but unable to pay their bills. Even though I really loved what I was called to do, I had responsibilities, as we all do.

I feel asleep, and suddenly I was transported to a different land, one filled with thousands, if not millions, of people. They were clustered around an East Indian guru; one of the bystanders told me that he was an expert at manifesting. Everyone was pushing and pulling to get close to him to discover the secret to prosperity.

Even in my dream, I thought, "Aha!" I forcefully elbowed my way through the crowd until I could look into the guru's eyes. I then asked him, "What's the secret to manifesting?"

He did not answer me, so I tried again—and again and again and again, while he ignored me. Finally, I got right in his face and shouted my question. And he responded.

"It's to be who you are with all your heart," he said, and I awoke.

I committed to my intuitive work and each stage that followed, eventually teaching classes, writing books, and presenting seminars. My family did not approve. Despite the resistance, I followed my heart. A few years later, a strange event underscored the wisdom from the dream.

A friend of mine invited me to a seminar on manifesting, led by the guru who had taught Dr. Wayne Dyer, an internationally renowned author and speaker in the field of self-development, how to manifest. The guru was the man in my dream. I sat in the first row and listened to everything he said, which reduced to the same statement he had made in my dream. You must, you *must*, be yourself. That is the key to manifesting.

### In the end, is it better to be paid for our work?

In a Bible story, Jesus admonishes a young man that to enter the kingdom of heaven, he must give up his wealth and belongings. Buddhist tradition speaks of detachment from everything, including money. Hindu teachings instruct followers in breathing and meditating so that they might free themselves from the physical world. These and other secular and spiritual groups insist that money is one of the many paths to evil. Is this true?

This misunderstanding of scripture and spiritual principles leads many people to believe that the purest of purposes involves being unpaid or giving away their time and talents. These traditions underscore the need to have no attachment to physical works—to live in the world but be not of it, as Jesus instructs.

My interpretation of the biblical story of Jesus's advice to the rich young man is that we must release everything we idolize. Some of us treasure money before goodness. Others place alcohol, sex, clothing, employment, emotionalism, houses, or chocolate before spiritual practice. Still others confuse religion with spirituality, thinking that God loves those best who have memorized the most Bible verses, bombed the most abortion clinics, or blown up the most heretics.

Ideally, Buddhists consider it important to pay their bills, as do the Sufis. Christians break bread with their fellow man and woman, no matter their race, creed, or religion. Muslims of heart pray for the Jewish people. Native Americans on American reservations thank their white brothers that learn their sacred ways.

The Jewish Talmud states that the first question asked of the deceased at the Heavenly Court will be this: "Did you conduct your business in a fair manner?" In this way, Jews are to perform *tikkun olam*, elevating the mundane to the holy.

There is nothing good or bad about making or having money. The ultimate goal—the true work—of money is to elevate the earthly to the heavenly. If we are doing this, we are making love, not money.

# Blocks and Challenges

## Why don't people automatically live on-purpose?

There are *many* reasons that make it hard to express our purpose. These include the following:

**Family of origin problems:** We are raised in a system where most of our family systems are unhealthy. Mom and Dad are not living their own dreams and might, in fact, dread being around anyone who is.

Maybe Mom buried her own purpose, and to compensate, she has become an alcoholic. How do you think she would react to a newcomer—a child—that has the gift of telling the truth? Perhaps Dad hates his job and resents taking care of the family. Is he really going to help his child follow his or her own star? Fortunately, many of my clients went beyond their family systems, sometimes even breaking with them in order to uncover and express their true selves.

**Lack of support:** Look around. How many people in your immediate family love what they do or who they are? How many people at your workplace, in your neighborhood, or at your local grocery store feel supported in what they do? It is easier to fly freely on the wings of our spirit if surrounded by people devoted to the same.

**Gender bias:** In general, society divides spiritual gifts into two categories: those acceptable for men and those applicable to women. You are in trouble if your calling requires access to the "other" side.

There are two sets of chakras and therefore two sets of spiritual gifts. These are the incoming and outgoing gifts. The even-numbered chakras are receiving centers in that they absorb energy from outside of the self and generate the more emotional, relational, and spiritual gifts. The related gifts are more creative and concentrate on feelings, love, and healing. These chakras and their corresponding gifts are usually considered feminine in nature. The odd-numbered chakras are outgoing in that when they are activated, they involve "pushing" energy into the world. Related gifts involve manifesting, thinking, communicating, and commanding. These areas are most typically associated with acceptable masculine traits.

Society originally drew a line between masculine and feminine chakras because of tribal mentality. Men are physically stronger and had to access the powerful and dominating chakras in order to keep the clan alive. Women were responsible for the children and therefore needed to draw upon the more creative and relational chakras and gifts. While this demarcation might have served the human race at one time, currently, these distinctions are not only unimportant but are sacrificial. World peace and personal success are only possible if every person contributes his or her unique gifts. Formulas no longer guarantee security.

**Cultural norms:** Society has a lot of rules. If you are Jewish, you need to pray a certain way; if you are Muslim, yet another. Rich people should do different things with their money than poor people. These and all artificial strictures inhibit the opening of one's individual chakras and, therefore, gifts. Being "normal" will never help you be who you really are.

**Personal fear:** Fear prevents us from expressing our authentic self. It actually tells us it is dangerous to be who we really are. Living in fear also thwarts our ability to empathize with others. True work is about love in action. If we cannot connect with others or ourselves, we will not be able to live purposefully.

**Relationship agreements:** Most relationships restrict rather than promote growth—especially traditional spousal relationships. Many women continue to believe that they belong at home, nurturing children and managing the house. While some women are spiritually called to be homemakers and most spend a good part of their lives raising children, this philosophy can inhibit the expansion of gifts that are not utilized in the home environment. This can emotionally penalize women who are successful at full-time jobs.

Men are supposed to be breadwinners, the contemporary version of hunting game, serving as warriors to protect the family. This ideal has resulted in a startling statistic. Despite the fact that most women are employed in jobs outside of the house, husbands continue to leave the majority of child and home care to their wives. This overload of work obviously stresses women—but how do men lose out? It means that men cannot access their so-called feminine chakras and gifts; they are therefore "stuck" in only one-half of themselves. Many households are challenging this traditional thinking with shared-power arrangements. This is especially true in same-sex partnerships, single-parent households, and families that follow non-fundamental religions.

**Defiance:** Some people refuse to conform to anything or anyone, literally throwing their own gifts away as easily as it is to throw trash in the garbage. I worked with one client who was so highly gifted at math, he received scholarship offers at several large universities. He did not take any of them, preferring to work as a janitor in a school. Why? His dad was an accountant, and he did not want to grow up to be like his father.

**Soul fears:** We carry experience in our souls, often across several lifetimes. If we were persecuted for employing our spiritual gifts in a different lifetime, we might believe we will be punished again.

## How do past-life experiences impact my ability to fulfill my current destiny?

Our soul is imprinted with the experiences we have undergone in this and other lifetimes. This is awesome—if those experiences were positive. Many clients report that they know how to play music, perform healings, take care of children, or use any other number of gifts because they can recall having done so before. In fact, children sometimes awaken with former capabilities. One of my clients, who did not believe in psychic "mumbo jumbo," changed her mind when her three-year-old would wake up dancing. The complexity of her ballet moves proved that she did, in fact, remember having been a ballerina in a previous lifetime, a statement made by the little girl.

Time and time again, clients express anxiety at the thought of living purposefully, as they remember being judged, banished, shamed, or killed for using the same gifts in an earlier incarnation. A classic example is a woman from Oregon who worked with me over the phone. She was an amazing healer; as soon as she put her hands on a client, the client would tremble, and often the presenting physical ailment would alleviate or completely disappear.

With great regret, however, my client had retired from her healing practice. Her work was accompanied by violent migraines that took two to three days' worth of recovery time.

Using my psychic vision, I immediately perceived a scene in the Middle Ages. My client was a midwife to a queen, who was in labor. As I watched, the baby died. In his grief, the king had my client beaten to death. The first blow was to her head. As my client's soul left her then-body, it decided that it would never use its gifts again.

My client's soul had held onto this memory and was now using the migraines as a self-protective device. Once we updated her soul's perception of reality, my client released her fear. She was able to resume her healing work, without the penalty of migraines.

### What about soul curses and cords? How might they affect my work success?

The soul is often laden with energetic bindings that restrict its movement, free will, and self-expression. Souls often carry these bindings from one lifetime to another, although this energy may also have formed in this lifetime.

Bindings are energetic limits that curb our spiritual self. They force a connection to unhealthy people, reinforce unhealthy patterns, and streamline negative thoughts that can inhibit our ability to take risks or accept success.

There are many types of negative bindings. These include the following:

**Curses:** A curse is a malevolent wish for harm that creates toxic situations. Usually, one person places it on another person, although a group, a spirit, or a group of spirits can also initiate it.

**Cords:** Cords look like psychic garden hoses that connect two people in an unhealthy way. A cord was the problem in the case of a twenty-five-year-old male client who was a farmer but wanted to be a doctor. Any time he even thought of taking pre-med classes, his throat would close up.

Using his own clairvoyant ability, my client perceived a cord between himself and his father, from whom he had inherited the farm. The father was deceased. Whenever the son thought about being a doctor, the father strangled him with a psychic cord. Through our work, we removed this cord, and the son is now in medical school—without a noose around his neck.

**Energy markers:** An energy marker appears psychically like a big X on a part of someone's body. It screams, "Treat me a certain way!"

Others accommodate. One of my clients had an energy marker that said, "Take advantage of me." It worked. Even though he was forty years old, my client spent most of his work time running errands for his boss. We removed the energy marker, and my client started his own business. He used his previous experience and entered the personal services business, and now he makes great money running errands for others—but as his own boss.

**Codependent bargains:** A codependent bargain is a cord that insists that we have to sacrifice a vital part of our self to get something we need in return. Usually, we end up giving ourselves away and getting nothing back.

## What role does my self-esteem play in achieving success?

Many of us inhibit our success because of self-doubt, low self-esteem, and limited self-confidence. These three restrictions are different but can be equally challenging.

**Self-doubt** strikes when we believe that we have nothing to offer the world. Many of us were treated as if we were unimportant when we were children. The only way to heal self-doubt is to understand the role it plays in our lives.

Self-doubt has a protective purpose. We doubt ourselves if we are afraid to fail at something that is important to us—such as our true work. The thinking goes like this:

*as long as I doubt myself, I don't have to try. If I do not try, I cannot fail at achieving my dreams. So I will keep my dreams hidden in my heart. That way, I will not have to find out that I am incapable of accomplishing them.*

**Self-esteem** refers to our relationship with self. A low self-esteem means that we do not like ourselves.

Many of us dislike ourselves because we weren't loved, appreciated, or affirmed when we were growing up. The unconscious benefit to self-loathing is that we cannot be rejected. If we do not connect with other people, go for the job we desire, leave a bad marriage, or ask out the person we really like, then we cannot be turned down. The truth is that we are going to fall flat on our faces as many times as we fly on our wings, but we'll never get off the ground if we don't try. We might be rejected by one company but accepted by another. Isn't our potential worth the effort?

**Self-confidence** describes our relationship with the world. Are we willing to take risks? Some of us limit our expansion into the world because we think we will be judged. We do not want to enter the water until we have already mastered the swan dive—and have a guaranteed audience of clapping enthusiasts.

Waiting for success until we have succeeded is not only impossible, it is delusional. A child does not know how to walk until he falls, repeatedly. Success is a process, and we will look stupid, trip, and stumble at various points in our lives. We also learn and become more proficient over time.

Expecting the full support of those around us is also impractical. Some people will help regardless. We all need a support system, usually referred to as friends. When we become more and more successful, there will be more audible detractors as well.

People become jealous. It is always easier to tear someone else apart than challenge ourselves.

Success and happiness also suggest that others could accomplish their own personal goals. If we took risks, so can others. If we willingly sacrificed, others could do the same. One person's accomplishments invites others to ask why they have not taken the risks necessary to become as accomplished, and that can be threatening.

### How do you, as a clairvoyant, determine someone's block to success?

I use my psychic vision to check for blocks. I usually see the blocks in someone's chakras or auric field.

Energetic blocks usually present themselves as discolored, dark, muddy, or malformed energies. Brackish energy in the first chakra, located in the groin area, indicates a problem manifesting. A tight fifth chakra, in the throat, indicates an inability to fully communicate. Sometimes energy is missing; for instance, I might perceive a missing auric layer. If the third layer is not where it is supposed to be, I know that the client is struggling in the areas of mental acuity and organization.

Once I spot the troubled area, I ask the Divine to clue me in on the specific causal issue. At this point, I might see a face in the middle of a chakra. Maybe Mom's head appears, and she is yelling. This tells me that Mom's anger is creating a problem for my client. Perhaps I picture an intense abusive situation, such as a rape or a violent act. I now ask the client if such an event occurred and how he or she has been affected.

I also ask to envision the solution to a challenge. Maybe sexual abuse closed down a client's first chakra and has restricted his or her ability to make money. The Divine is usually more than happy to provide me an image to assist. I might picture the business card of a therapist who can help my client deal with the original trauma. Perhaps I will visualize a color that my client should wear in order to help clear the negative energies. I have learned that we carry our histories in color, shape, and form throughout our lives, and that it is our right not only to decipher the stories but to rewrite them for happier endings.

## How can I evaluate my blocks to success?

There are many ways to uncover the blocks keeping us from living our destiny. Here are a few:

**Work with a therapist or spiritual director:**
Sometimes we need to journey to the past with a loving guide, one who can help us reclaim our inner purity and set new goals for the future.

**Look to the soul:** There are many ways to revisit the past to release the anchors that keep us from sailing forward. When meditating, ask to envision the past life that is causing a current problem. When journaling, begin with the phrase "once upon a time," and allow your soul to step forward and write the story that is dampening your success. Conduct a regression with a shaman or hypnosis expert.

**Dream a dream:** When going to bed at night, ask the Divine to send you a dream that will explain your current discomfort. Make sure you have pen and paper near your bed and record what you receive.

**Draw your own conclusions:** Grab a picture of the human body and create a timeline of situations that might be adversely affecting your work success. Let your intuition guide you as you record the various events, situations, and feelings that might be creating today's difficulties. Write your conclusions on the parts of the body most affected, and then, when meditating, ask these bodily regions to provide you more of the story.

**Divine the Divine:** Pray. Ask the Divine for information and for healing.

# The Spiritual World and Work

## What spiritual beings help us with our spiritual purpose?

We all have spiritual guides. As explained in various sections of this book, angels, ancestors, the deceased, and any number of interplanetary and natural beings, as well as interdimensional forces, attend us. Any and all of these can and do assist us with achieving our destiny. In reference to our work, there are "specialist guides" that help us with our particular concerns; for example, a deceased doctor might attend a surgeon. The spirit world is very interwoven with our own. After all, our destiny is intertwined with others' destinies, so in helping us, the spirits help themselves.

## How do our ancestors positively impact our work success?

Ancestors and our ancestry can bolster our destiny in three ways.

First, we can inherit genes that enable our spiritual mission. Genetic encoding is not always the outcome of haphazard biological processes, as science asserts. Rather, our soul initiates a complex energetic process before birth, to select the genes that will best support our spiritual mission. Specifically, our ninth chakra, which carries our soul genes, works with our tenth chakra, the grounding center, to choose physical genes that will assist our life purpose.

Second, ancestral memories are recorded in our bodies and can be used to help us negotiate life. A newer branch of science called epigenetics is proving that we inherit memories and experience from our ancestors. These are carried in the chemical "soup" surrounding our DNA.

Third, your ancestors might still be hanging around, providing you with advice and insight. Almost all my clients insist that spirits surround them. The majority of these guides are angelic or ancestral. One of my clients refuses to make a move in her housecleaning business without talking to her deceased grandmother Marie, who kept a spotless house. Another client, a professor in a veterinary school, has daily conversations in his head with his deceased grandfather, who was a cattle farmer.

## Can my ancestors inhibit my success?

Not every "dead person," or ancestral energy, wants the best for us. This plays out in three main ways.

First, we do not always end up with the genes we really want or need. One factor is chance and circumstance. We might accidentally inherit the gene for bipolar disorder despite our best-laid soul plans and end up being too emotional to succeed at work without medication. Another factor is human error. Maybe Mom married the "wrong person" and we lack the necessary genetic alphabet to write the story we desired.

Sometimes malevolent entities deliberately interfere with the conception process. One might slip in a gene we do not want, leaving us without the bone structure we need to be a gymnast or the intellect necessary to become a professor.

Are we doomed to suffer if the spirits work against us? No. The Divine makes use of everything we have gone through, even the most terrible of mistakes. I once worked with a woman who thought that a negative ancestor had cursed her birthing process. When born, she was a "blue baby," lacking in oxygen. The result was a learning disability that had plagued her entire life.

My client did not believe that she had contracted for this problem. Through our work, she determined that her grandmother's soul had hexed her birth in an attempt to trade places with my client. My client had refused to abdicate her body, so the grandmother's soul had constricted the umbilical cord in retaliation. Over time, my client was able to incorporate the learning disability into her destiny plan, however. A musician, she went back to school and became a musical therapist, using music to teach children with learning challenges.

Second, the epigenetic "brew" of our ancestral memories can serve up detrimental as well as positive fears and inhibitions. For instance, my mother's parents survived the Depression. When working with the chemical imprints around my DNA, I literally felt everything they went through during their toughest years as farmers in North

Dakota. I discovered that I had spent most of my life listening to my grandmother's conclusion: God had abandoned her. As I sent her healing, I also released the negative belief from my own body. I was able to see that she
and my grandfather had endured the Depression because
of the Divine, not in spite of the Divine. The resulting
faith has enabled me to take life-affirming risks in love,
parenting, and work.

Third, not every ghostly ancestor wishes us well. For
many years, I worked with a woman who was the third
generation to be an administrator for a steel union. Her
grandfather would frequently visit her, handing out sage
advice. Her deceased father, however, was so jealous of
his father's success that he sabotaged my client. The father
would literally hide contracts that were on her desk. One
minute, they would be there—the next, they were gone
forever. We helped my client's father release his pain and
rage, and my client's work problems cleared up. She never
"lost" another contract.

## Do the deceased continue to serve a purpose, even from the other side?

All conscious beings have purpose, whether in-body or
out of body, whether dead or alive. We actually pursue the
same destiny plan on both sides.

After death, we continue our spiritual mission through
journeying on one of several pathways, or levels of awareness. I call these the Planes of Light, the subject of my
book *Illuminating the Afterlife*.

## Can a departed loved one serve his or her purpose by visiting me?

Yes, and chances are, you are often surrounded by loved ones who have departed this realm before you. In fact, when you're dead, your own spiritual mission will probably involve interacting with living loved ones.

The veil between worlds is gossamer thin. It is not hard for a soul to reach—and sometimes pop—through from the other side. Often a soul must visit to fulfill a vital part of his or her mission. I once worked with a woman who ran an orphanage in South America. The spirit of a doctor who had worked at a nearby medical clinic before his death frequently visited her.

My uncle often visits me, despite the fact that he died a few years ago. Mike had been our family physician and would often make home visits when my sisters or I were sick. Sometimes, he even made "animal calls." I still remember the time he diagnosed Snoopy, my white rat, using a stethoscope and thermometer. He stepped away from the ailing animal and pronounced him sick with a cold.

## Does suicide destroy someone's path of destiny?

No; in fact, I have determined that the soul of a suicide victim usually becomes a guide for the living, often assisting other troubled individuals with their problems. I once worked with a support group of dozens of families who had lost their children to suicide, and the souls of nearly every departed child returned to show me the great work they were doing to help the living.

## How might the deceased help me determine my spiritual purpose?

Those who have walked this plane often like to help the living fulfill their destinies. One of my favorite stories on this topic involves a plumber who was tired of his career. Although he had spent thirty successful years in the plumbing trade, my client was sad. He had never wanted to become a plumber. He did not feel brave enough to make a change, however, and asked for my insight.

The first picture I perceived was of an older gentleman holding an instrument. I had no idea what the tool did. The older man, dressed in overalls, obviously understood my dilemma because he winked at me and then plunged the metallic instrument into a toilet. Even I could understand the point. I asked my client if his father had been a plumber and if so, if that was how he got his start in the business.

My client nodded and began to tear up. "Is my father here?" he asked. The man in my mind nodded, and I said yes.

My client proceeded to hold a conversation with his father through me, finally asking the most important question: "Dad, would you be disappointed in me if I changed professions?" In my mind's eye, the father began crying and shaking his head, as if saying no.

Finally I asked my client what he wanted to do with his life. His facial features fell, and he admitted that he did not know, whereupon his father sent me a new picture.

I saw a vision of a young boy scribbling with crayons, sketching one picture after another. In my head, I asked the father if this image portrayed his son's real calling. The father nodded.

I relayed the vision to the son, who looked shocked. "Why, I've always wanted to be an artist, but my father told me I couldn't pay my bills if I pursued that path!"

In my head, the father leaned over his son and patted his back. I had the strong sense that the father wanted to repair the damage he had done to his son.

A few years later, I received a message on my voice mail. My client, with his wife's support, had taken classes in design and graphics. He had just handed over his plumbing business to his daughter—who loved it—and started a small graphic design business in his basement.

### Does the Divine help us achieve our destiny?

I have countless stories that underscore the loving, hands-on care of the Divine. Here is one involving a client who tried to commit suicide.

This client had been in the Russian Mafia his entire life. He was so out of touch with his authentic self that he had even encouraged his own son to join the group. A few years later, the son was killed by an opposing organization.

My client was devastated. He knew that at some level, it was his fault that his son had died. He took his gun, locked himself in his car, wrote a note to his wife, and shot himself.

He knows that the gun went off. He not only heard it, he felt the ripping pain through his head. He waited for the lights to go off. Instead, a light brighter than any he had ever seen appeared before him, and he heard a voice say the following: "My son, do not give up on yourself. I have not."

The pain suddenly disappeared, and my client opened his eyes. He was still holding the gun, but there were no bullets missing. Had he imagined the scenario? Dreamed it all? A few days later, he received a call from a missionary, who suggested that he give up his work and start working within the orphanage system to find homes for the lost. My client had no idea how the missionary got his number, but he felt brave enough to walk away from the Mafia and start a new career.

# Work and the World Around Us

## Do animals and other natural beings have work or a soul purpose?

Most native communities believe that many natural beings have souls and their own individual missions. This includes animals, reptiles, birds, and many native life forms and objects, including plants, trees, rocks, and water. What makes natural beings different from human beings is that most also interconnect through a species-based spirit.

For instance, all individual tigers—dead or alive—communicate through a greater tiger spirit. All spiders connect through a spider spirit. This larger spirit serves as a guide and a net, catching the soul at death and then re-releasing it when it's time to be born again.

## Does every natural being or object have a purpose?

Not every natural force is animate or conscious. Some natural energies are the byproduct of something greater. For instance, a breeze might result from a wind—or perhaps the angry roar of a lion. A breeze might produce a change in an animate being, as when it gently lifts the hat off a person's head, but that does not mean it directed this change.

Some natural entities or energies might have been conscious once but have lost their consciousness over time. I once stumbled into a forest in the Sierra de Aralar region of Spain that was replete with conscious and unconscious natural entities. Some of the rocks and trees literally spoke to my friends and myself; they told stories I felt within my bones and could write onto paper. Yet other rocks littering the site were sightless and soundless.

## Can a human soul occupy a natural object or being?

Sometimes destiny calls for an exchange between a human soul and the natural world. And sometimes souls end up in the strangest places because of strange occurrences.

I once spent two weeks traveling across the British Isles, investigating sacred sites. I happened upon a stone circle and was standing near one of the stones when I heard a cry.

I looked around but could not see anyone. The sound continued. I heard breathing—and words. They seemed to be emanating from one of the standing stones! I put my ear closer and heard communication from a wizard, who had apparently been locked in the stone by a competitor. I asked the Divine to free the wizard from his prison and help him continue his soul path.

## What might make a soul leave its natural habitat, such as a tree soul leave its home tree?

A being's soul—and this includes a human being's soul—might depart its body for many reasons. All lives run their course. Eventually, we all die. Death is nothing more or less than a soul leaving the body to continue the path of destiny in a different way.

Sometimes, however, the physical body—whether it is a human body or some other natural form—continues to operate, even though the soul has left. We have all met people who look, seem, and act as if alive, but feel "dead." They are not "here." We might experience these people as checked out, cold, mean, or even sociopathic. This might point to one of several conditions:

1.  The soul is actually absent, and nothing has taken its place.
2.  Part of the soul is gone, and nothing fills the empty space.
3.  Part or all of the soul is leaving, and something else now occupies that space. Usually this something else is not very nice. It might be an entity or a network of entities, a demon, a deceased ancestor, or even a negative part of that person's soul.

If any of these situations have occurred, the original soul will not be able to completely fulfill his or her destiny.

Beings in nature can be affected by the same condition. Tree spirits or souls often flee if their forest is about to be felled by loggers or burned by wildfire. A tree soul might hide in the roots or a small part of the trunk if too many humans crowd into its ecosystem. A fish might swim about fully conscious until it perceives it is about to be caught. Its soul will withdraw before being hooked or netted.

Native peoples knew that natural beings have spirit. This is why they would pray to the Great Spirit before hunting, requesting that they be presented only with the animals ready to leave this world. Before killing the hunted, they would thank the animal's spirit for its sacrifice. Because of this, the meat was not tainted by fear and the animal's spirit could more easily reenter the world.

### What are some purposes served by various natural beings and objects?

Here are some of the more typical purposes served by different natural beings and objects:

> **Rocks:** Serve as historians, keepers of information and history; they hold and direct energy.

> **Trees:** Conduct communication, share information with other trees, even those not in immediate vicinity; can convey messages among different species.

> **Flowers:** Each reflects a different type of energy, which invites and amplifies healing, creativity, manifesting, or another endeavor.

> **Grass:** Holds and distributes energy from the stars.

> **Planets and stars:** Each conscious planet or star reflects a significant truth or virtue.

> **Water:** Reflects energies in or around it.

**Birds:** Represent various aspects of freedom, vision, and movement.

**Reptiles:** Carry various energies needed for transformation.

**Animals:** Each represents a different expression of life; for instance, bears are strength, deer share love, dogs offer loyalty and friendship, and cats are sensuality and cunning.

## What are examples of the work conducted by companion animals?

I will begin by explaining that I have been investigating this phenomenon through the desires of my youngest son, Gabriel. To date, the mini-zoologist has formed a community that has included two dogs, one cat, two turtles, a rabbit, a guinea pig, and a mealworm. And there were the five goldfish—named Spiderman, Zach, Fish, Cody, and Superman.

I can testify to the persnickety individuality of these beings' purposes; not only is each his or her own personality, but each serves a unique mission in the pantheon of the household. Honey (already introduced in Part I) considers himself the sole proprietor of Gabriel's time. We are not sure if he thinks himself a boy saddened by the cruel lack of tails on other boys or a dog with a tail living among dogs without tails. Whatever the case, he has his own pillow on Gabe's bed and has been known to whisper in Gabe's ear that he wants a nightly story or he can't fall asleep (Gabe relays this message for Honey). At any rate, Honey is really around to serve Gabe, and he has loved Gabe through all the normal and aggravated experiences of childhood. He is, succinctly, Gabe's best friend.

Coco is a deaf and blind dog that was abandoned on the highway. Coco is a shaman. Tuned out to reality, she nonetheless finds the people who need healing and settles them into perfect well-being.

Johnny T. Cat turns up every time a client or household visitor is emotional, at which time he purrs the hurt away. I think of him as God as a cat.

Max the guinea pig is the warning system, chirping every time something is about to go wrong, and Wilma the turtle is the boss of the kitchen.

### Can something as small as a butterfly have a purpose?

A young girl asked me this sweet question, and I had to laugh before replying yes. She looked at me, puzzled, before asking the next logical question: "How do you know?" To which I replied, "I know because a butterfly once told me."

I was sitting on my front steps one summer, thinking about Jesus Christ and wondering if he only came to earth to communicate with people or if he was also connected to the beings of nature. I suddenly felt his presence.

It was as if he entered me, and I heard his voice say, "This is the seventh dimension, my favorite one, for through it, I can communicate with all."

At that point, the world of a Midwestern suburban lawn transformed into its own poetic universe. I could hear the grass swish, swish, and imagined it singing to the Divine—or perhaps, singing the Divine. I would translate the lyrics as "all love, all love," but that is a narrow interpretation of the beautiful verse. Even though it was daylight, I could hear the stars above the cloud-plain as they received the song of the grass and offered their own bright and dazzling response in return, which sounded something like "more love, more love."

Every beetle and mosquito seemed alive and conscious. The tiniest of flowers nodded its head in personality and purpose. However, the most enjoyable individual I met that day was a butterfly.

A monarch butterfly, orange and black, landed on my right hand. It fluttered softly, and I was awed by its choice of me as a landing strip.

"Are you a butterfly?" I asked it, aloud.

"No," was the vehement answer, accompanied by a flap of wings so loud, I knew I must have irritated this "little man."

"I'm a Yakowitz."

"A Yakowitz?" I asked, taken aback.

"A Yakowitz," he responded, firmly. As if still miffed, he wiggled toward the end of my finger, preparing to fly away.

"I'm sorry," I offered quickly, not wanting to end the conversation. "I didn't think—"

"No, you did not," he huffed. "As if PEOPLE knew the names of NOT PEOPLE."

I thought he made a good point. Not wanting to strain our relationship further than it already was, I changed tracks.

"What do Yakowitzes do?" I queried.

"Oh, we're very important," he stated.

"Why?" I wondered aloud. "Do you pollinate the flowers?"

I had once again stuck my foot in my mouth, for Mr. Yakowitz fluttered his wings quite furiously. He must have decided not to hold my humanness against me, for he then filled me in.

"The flowers are nothing compared to the Yakowitzes," he pronounced. "They are merely receptacles for information. It's my job to leave messages for—"

(At this point, I could not understand the exact names provided by my informant, for Yakowitz names are not humanly pronounceable or even understandable to the limited human ear and brain. Therefore, I substitute purely American names for those originally provided.)

"—Betty Yakowitz from Bob Yakowitz about what Bubba Yakowitz was doing with Bertha Yakowitz when Bernie Yakowitz was supposed to be watching Bernice Yakowitz's child, Barb."

In other words, the Yakowitzes are the great gossipers of nature.

And with that, Mr. Yakowitz flew off.

As you might surmise from my story, every living being has purpose, including the butterflies.

## What are examples of purpose in the plant kingdom?

A few years ago, a shaman named Don Hermon in Peru asked if I was interested in meeting his healing teacher. On behalf of the group I was leading, I said yes. We paddled upriver to a small clearing on the bank of the Black River.

We stared ahead into the foliage, our hearts dropping. It was so thick that it looked nearly black. But no—there was an overgrown path. Almost. We followed Don Hermon and a young boy with a machete and a rifle into the heart of darkness.

After what seemed like hours, we stopped in another clearing, where we faced a great and grand tree. To me, it looked just like the Tree of Life in Disney's Animal Kingdom in Orlando. Others might have compared it more favorably and religiously to the trees mentioned in the Garden of Eden story of the Old Testament. At any rate, Don Hermon turned to the group, and with a tear in one of his eyes, said, "This is my teacher. I've been studying with her for eight years."

At first, it did not seem like the tree was alive. How could it perform as instructor, leader, and healer? Then, one of our members ventured close, and I sensed a reaction in the tree. Intuitively, I knew that the tree had decided to teach a lesson to this woman, one that she probably would not appreciate, but which I was not supposed to judge. Suddenly a swarm of small black insects flew from the tree and surrounded her, biting her. She screamed and began to run around as red pustules sprang up on her skin.

Don Hermon stood by placidly, and I knew that I had been ushered into a tutorial of my own. The tree sent me a picture, that of me spreading a balm over the woman's inflamed body in order to heal her. Quickly, I searched through my knapsack. I had no such cream. No magic potion. No baby powder. What did I find? I pulled out a small jar of lip balm and felt the tree respond.

Lip balm? I thought. The vision from the tree intensified. I went to the stricken woman and began to rub the lip balm over her body, whispering that I had brought a healing lotion with me that would instantly relieve the condition. Without a question, she calmed down, and the red pustules disappeared.

The tree waved her branches in satisfaction.

What did I learn? That the tree has a purpose, and that part of her purpose as teacher was to reveal the power of belief. I did nothing special. I did not even believe that the lip balm would do anything. But the patient believed she'd be healed—and so did the tree.

# Determining Your Purpose

## How did you learn about your own spiritual work?

I had two dreams that revealed my ultimate purpose. I received them over two nights when journeying through Morocco.

At the beginning of the trip, I asked the Divine to disclose my purpose. That night was New Year's Eve. Three friends, including my favorite travelling companion, Cathy, and myself had been rerouted through London to land in Casablanca later than we had originally expected. Our luggage, asserting its independence, had strayed to Barcelona. There we were, four beds in one room, sharing Pete's clothes, for his was the only bag that had arrived in a timely fashion.

The first dream opened like a play in my parent's house. The house was dark and dreary. No matter what I did, I could not produce enough light to see clearly. My childhood home environment had been exactly like this. In the dream, I struck out on my own, just as I had when I was nineteen, seeking a better way to live.

In the dream, I ended up at a school. This was not your normal school; rather, it was outdoors under a canopy of clouds and rainbows. The teacher was God, a man dressed in khaki pants, a white shirt, and red tennis shoes. His back to me, he was drawing a picture of the universe that showed the track of planets, suns, and moons.

At some point, he drew a circle around the entirety and made a few chalk *X*'s outside of the sphere. He then turned to me.

"Your job is to label what's outside of reality."

I was a bit shocked. How was I supposed to know what lay outside of the known universe? In dismay, I responded, "How will I know?"

Now God did a very uncharacteristic God thing, at least according to my religious upbringing.

"Make it up," he said.

I was not too sure I wanted to take that one on, so I replied the following way: "What if I don't want to?"

"I will get someone else to do it," he said, before returning to his drawing.

I accepted the assignment.

This dream outlined my general purpose, which is to label the unknown, or the subtle reality. I do not really "make things up," although some people—those who don't hear the inaudible, see the invisible, or sense the not-provable—have insisted that I do. I actually attune to what is not there to explain what should be there.

As somewhat clarifying as this dream was, it did not completely explain the benefit of my work. The next night, I dreamed the answer to this question.

In the second dream, I was strolling through sand dunes wearing my adventure clothing. In front of me were buildings. None were higher than one or two stories and all were colored burnt orange, the same hue as the landscape.

A young man appeared out of nowhere and began to walk with me, introducing himself with a statement: "Thank you."

"Thank you for what?" I asked, surprised that someone would even talk to me.

"For this," he said, waving his hand over the panorama, which was a business center as well as a village.

I asked what I had to do with the buildings, and he explained that my work had enabled thousands, if not millions, of people to find their true work and thus, begin their own businesses. I was surprised at the exponential effect of my work, especially when I entered the village and arrived at my own office, which was without a doubt the smallest office in the entire complex.

I owned a small shop, which was so narrow that it was hard to turn around in it. There was a set of stools, perhaps three or four, against a countertop, arranged like a diner. There was a single, clear case that featured only one item: a pair of eyeglasses. A mirror stood nearby.

There was an immense queue of people lined up outside my office. When a new "customer" would enter, I would take the eyeglasses out of its case, place them on his or her nose, and help them look into the looking glass. I would utter only one set of instructions: "See yourself the way that God sees you."

The client would suddenly shudder and inevitably begin to glow. His or her true self acknowledged, the client would leave, and another would sit on the stool and put on the glasses.

Now I knew the benefit I would provide others. Using my clairvoyance, I could enable them to see themselves the way that God sees them. The resulting flooding of love would invite healing, self-awareness, and an acceptance of spiritual purpose. Understanding their mission, individuals would then be able to offer their gifts to the world.

## What do you think is the key to opening to purpose?

I do not think we can reach for the future before we heal the past. Imagine a tree. For the branches to reach to the sky, strong enough to hold the birds, bees, butterflies, and other forms of life, it needs deep and strong roots. The roots are our past, which must be cleansed and opened to allow the sun to nurture our growth so we can support what we need to do.

## How do you help others evaluate their purpose?

There are many techniques. Here is what I would advise:

1. Believe that you are on this planet at this time to serve a vital purpose. The Divine wants you here. Others need you here. You are uniquely equipped to meet the needs of this world in only the way that you can.

2. Clear the past. Look at where you have come from. You will continue the same path unless you restore yourself through grace, analyzing for blocks, forgiving the mistakes, and accepting the lessons.

3. Ask for divine help. We are incarnate. The body is our vehicle for generating love into the physical plane. It is also restrictive. It holds our soul and is filled with and encompassed by our spirit, but it is still impermanent and partial to ideas that might not be accurate. By asking for divine assistance, your intuitive faculties can provide the information, insight, and healing necessary to make wise decisions.

4. Determine the truth. Specifically, isolate which spiritual truths you are here to represent—and become. Use the Internet to search virtues or other value-based terms, and decide which two or three best describe you. Ask yourself: What three concepts do I live for? What three concepts am I willing to die for? These indicate the spiritual truths you are here to integrate through your spiritual work.

5. Analyze yourself for your spiritual gifts. Use the chakra-based information in this book or my many other books, including *Attracting Prosperity Through the Chakras*. Study the chakras.

I recommend my work and also that of Carolyn Myss, Harish Johari, and Anodea Judith. Read the apostle Paul's descriptions of the gifts in the Christian New Testament or study the Hindu concept of the *siddhi*. Embrace these gifts, and accept what they tell you about your spiritual mission.

6. Frame your mission. As shown in the next question, summarize your spiritual purpose.

7. Perform a vision quest. A vision quest is a tool for receiving spiritual guidance, which in turn can reveal your spiritual calling. Indigenous societies initiated their youngsters into the community through vision quests conducted over three days. After preparing, a young person was left alone outside, with no food or assistance. During that time, a guide, often in the guise of an animal, or "totem," would appear to present the youngster with a vision for his or her life. I encourage clients to perform their own vision quests but in a practical, creative way. Consider renting a room in a hotel and spending a few days meditating in an atmosphere outside your daily concerns.

8. Perform a regression. Allow a trusted spiritual director to lead you into the past. Visit pertinent past lives or the white zone to review what you have been and to reveal who you are.

9. Ride the wind—into the future. You can return to the past but also visit the future. With guidance, catch the breeze and fly forward a few years. What are you doing? What is your work? Now plan backwards.

10. Create a vision board. Cut pictures and phrases out of magazines, books, or newspapers that signify your dreams. Paste them on a board and look at the sum total every day. What you see, you can become.

11. Meditate. Every day, ask the Divine to send you messages and guidance. We all have an easier time getting somewhere when there are signs to follow.

12. Enjoy the process. Work is a process, not an event. You might as well have fun at it!

## How do I write a mission statement?

It is helpful to write a one- or two-sentence mission statement that keeps you focused on your purpose. In general, a spiritual purpose is made of three components:

1. Spiritual truths.

2. Use of gifts.

3. Effect on others.

**Spiritual truths** are stated as virtues such as faith, truth, love, honor, healing, and hope.

**Spiritual gifts** are the practical applications of these truths. The result of using our gifts is that we affect others, ultimately creating more love.

The easiest way to summarize our spiritual calling is to write a sentence or short paragraph constructed from the three components of spiritual work, which are listed in the preceding Q&A. I also like to add a reality-based statement that describes the professional outlet for the spiritual calling.

For example, I helped clients come up with the following statements:

> To uphold the truths of faith and healing by
>     sharing my gifts in compassion and love as a
>     therapist to others who need to restore faith
>     in themselves.

> To use my gifts in harmonizing and understanding
>     history in order to uphold the truths of
>     honesty and honor. I will do this in my work
>     as a military soldier who serves her country
>     so that others can lead peaceful lives.

And my own:

> To represent love, healing, and happiness
> to help people see themselves as God
> sees them by offering my gifts of
> vision, manifesting, shamanism, and
> communication as an energy healer.

THE *I* IN illness stands for isolation, and the crucial letters in wellness are *we*.

—Author unknown[2]

---

2  As quoted in Mimi Guarneri, *The Heart Speaks: A Cardiologist Reveals the Secret Language of Healing* (Touchstone, 2006).

# Q&A:
## Health

Health is wholeness. When we are healthy, we are in touch with the essential truth of our being.

A healthy person is not a perfect person; we each have issues and problems. Maybe we have trouble with our skin or are bothered with a limp or have to battle an even more disabling condition. Perhaps we struggle with emotional or mental health issues that are invisible physically or we are confused about our spiritual beliefs. These situations do not detract from our innate wholeness—if

- we are willing to accept our wholeness;
- we are willing to express our wholeness; and
- we are willing to communicate with
  others in wholesome ways.

This section is less about our physical well-being, the typical definition of health, and is more about our total well-being.

To explore the health and wholeness questions I most frequently hear in my work as a clairvoyant, I will concentrate on these primary topics: the meaning of health, physical health, emotional and mental health, and spiritual health.

Overall, the role of clairvoyance and intuition reminds me of a quote from a rare and old book that muses on the health of a visionary:

> OBJECT I : These seers are visionary and
> melancholy people, and fancy they see things that
> do not appear to them, or anybody else.

> ANSW: The people of these isles, and particularly the Seers,
> are very temperate, and their diet is simple and moderate
> in quantity and quality; so that their brains are not in all
> probability disordered by undigested fumes of meat or drink.
> Both sexes are free from hysteria fits, convulsions, and several
> other distempers of that sort; there is no madmen among them,
> nor any instance of self-murder. It is observed among them,
> that a man drunk never sees Second Sight; and he that is a
> visionary, would discover himself in other things as well...[3]

---

3 Theophilus Insulanus, *The Second Sight* (Edinburgh: Ruddiman, Auld, and Co., Printers, 1763), 183.

# The Meaning of Health

## What is health?

Most of us define health in physical terms. We equate it with physical fitness and strength. We usually think that people are healthy in the absence of illness, injury, or impairment, but this definition would mean that none of us is ever healthy.

Did you know that even now, you are afflicted with viruses, bacteria, and even cancer cells? The word *health* means "whole." We are always whole, for we are spiritual beings, made of several parts: physical, emotional, mental, and spiritual. The truly healthy person is the one who is able to acknowledge all parts of him- or herself despite challenging circumstances.

Our healthy self, our whole self, is actually the sum total of everything we have ever experienced: the hard and the easy, the pleasant and the unpleasant, and the neutral, whether caused by others or ourselves. Everything we are creates the self we have become.

## How do I become a healthier person?

It's okay to want to look, feel, and act better. Usually, however, people seeking better health just want to be more attractive physically.

So let's rephrase the question. Instead of asking about how to transform into a piece of fantasy, perhaps the inquiry should be how to become more authentic.

## What does authenticity have to do with health?

The term *authentic* means "original" and "genuine." You are an original. You are the only "you" that has ever been. If you express who you really are in all that you do, you are being authentic. You are being "you."

There is a second part to the formula: authenticating others. When you interact with another's true self, it validates your own true self. You can now express more of yourself and, therefore, be even more whole. You can live a balanced life, equally concerned about self and others.

## How do I live authentically?

Being healthy through authenticity is really about experiencing the Golden Rule: we are to treat others the way we want them to treat us.

On the surface, this does not seem difficult. My son Gabriel put it succinctly:

"This means that if I'm nice to others, they'll be nice back. Wow! That also means that if I give them what they want, they'll give me what I want."

There are a few qualifications. First, we cannot control others through our actions. Authenticity *does* start with treating ourselves in a good way, through behaviors and attitudes that increase our self-esteem, that actualize our value system, and that leave us feeling good about ourselves. If we want to develop into our best selves, we must be our best selves.

It is important to look at ourselves with kindness and forgiveness; to take care of our own needs; and to be gracious and ethical. If we treat ourselves poorly, as in eating too many jelly donuts for breakfast or mainlining heroin or loathing ourselves, we are going to treat other people in a similar fashion.

However, being good to ourselves does not mean that others will be good to us in return. We get what others choose to give us.

People who are cranky internally are going to be grumpy externally. We can't be sweet or affectionate or acquiescent just because we want someone to be the same in return. We have to be ourselves because it feels good to be just that. The authentic lifestyle demands that we draw the line between self and others and decide to be around people that *can* treat us in the way we deserve to be treated. In other words, authenticity begins with self-responsibility delivered with a detachment from expectations.

Only after we own full responsibility for our actions can we move to the second part of the authenticity formula, or the Golden Rule. When we are self-responsible, we can now be responsive toward others. We are able to see and behave toward them with respect and kindness, in a way that mirrors how we are with ourselves.

## Why don't I always treat myself very well?

Many of us are mean to ourselves. The truth is that we will treat ourselves the way that others have treated us until we decide to act differently.

Chances are, you behave toward yourself exactly the way that your parents acted toward you when you were growing up. If your mother constantly ignored your feelings, you will ignore your own feelings. If your dad drank a lot of alcohol, you will either drink to ignore your own needs or develop a comparable addiction.

If you look for the cause of your parents' behavior, you will see that your parents were treating you the way that their parents treated them. Most human actions are formulaic. Formulas can be changed.

When working with clients who ask about their health, I always ask for pictures to explain the reasons for the poor health, mental challenges, or emotional dissatisfaction. In almost every case, I see one or both of the parents performing activities that taught my client how to become self- (and/or other-) injurious. One of the clearest examples involved a man who came to see me because he had repetitive walking pneumonia.

It only took a few minutes to determine the most apparent reason he was sick all the time. He traveled internationally nearly every month and was constantly exposed to unhealthy air and food. In addition, the jet lag prevented him from restoring his immune system. I saw other pictures, however, that spoke to far more serious concerns.

First, I saw that every time he was overseas, he drank alcohol and took drugs. He also spent a lot of time in bars connecting with women. He admitted to these behaviors and explained that one of the reasons he was scared to treat the condition medically was that he did not want to admit his "midnight activities" to a doctor.

I was puzzled. This man's level of shame was high, but who or what had taught him that hurting himself in these ways was acceptable? I asked the Divine for more pictures, and a filmstrip emerged.

Not only was this man's marriage miserable, but it also mirrored his parents' marriage. The reason my client had not been able to evaluate the real source of his health issues was that he had adopted his mother's family role and married someone who acted like his father. My client's father was an addict; so was my client's wife. My client's mother had sacrificed herself—and her children—so her husband, who had power and money, would take care of her. My client, although he was a man, had gone through life doing the same. When his mother was under stress, she would drink, get sick, and flirt with men. My client had adapted to his mother's strategies for survival so well, he was living them out.

### How can I ever see myself as whole when I am feeling so broken?

I should really own stock in Kleenex, because most of my clients cry—and me along with them. What usually causes the breakdown? The fact that this always means my client is close to a breakthrough.

The irony is that before we can embrace our wholeness, the state of completion that is always present and true, we must also accept the brokenness that is within and often outside of ourselves.

Most of us have broken parts. Maybe we were shamed whenever we shared our opinions. Maybe parts of us were beaten down; maybe we were even literally beaten. Our essential self cannot be damaged, but our feelings can be bruised, our thoughts scattered and misaligned, our spiritual beliefs hidden and devalued. In an attempt to cope with life, many of us took these hurt and scattered parts of ourselves and glued them together inappropriately. We're still all there, just not quite put together in the right way. In other words, we're each a Ming vase—that's been cracked and repaired wrong.

To be restored, we have to be "taken apart" so we can be put together the "right way." The old paste has to be stripped and cleared, and a new adhesive applied. In place of the fears that have kept us together, we require the bonding material of the Holy Spirit, the Kuan Yin, the Divine, the Great All, or the Krishna.

In order to be put together in the "right order," we have to admit we're a little off our course. To accomplish this goal, I often advocate a twelve-step program, including Alcoholics Anonymous (AA) and Al-Anon, the program for codependents in relation to addictions. The first step on the road to recovery—on the path of living as whole people—is to admit that we have not done a very good job at running our own lives and need the help that can only be provided by the Divine.

# Physical Health

## Can I ever achieve perfect physical health?

Westerners believe that if you work hard enough, and use enough Listerine, toilet bowl cleaner, and starch, you can sanitize physical reality so thoroughly that germs don't stand a chance. As a caregiver to the small and powerful, I only have this to say: no matter how often I change the cat litter, it needs to be changed again.

There's always going to be something undermining physical perfection.

What if we were to desire physical *wholeness* rather than physical perfection? What if we were to establish goals for optimum rather than faultless health? We would relax, decreasing our stress. With less stress, our immune systems would function better. We would be sick less often, and we would feel like eating better and exercising more. Quite simply, living a wholesome life makes us feel and look better physically.

## What is optimum physical health?

None of us can achieve perfect physical health. We can, however, function at our optimum level. This is the highest level of physical, emotional, mental, and spiritual health possible for who we really are.

## What are the keys to achieving our optimum health?

There are two activities involved in becoming as healthy as possible. The first is hard work, and there is no substitute for it.

Clients often ask me for the key to physical fitness, and I always tell them that at one level, there is no mystery. You have to eat well, sleep a lot, and move your body. Period. You will not be as healthy and happy as you can possibly be if you skip these steps.

But there's another equally important ingredient, and that's spirituality. Our spirit is partnered with our body, and thus it is empowered to shape and direct our physical self. It needs our body healthy and honed if it is to carry out its spiritual purpose. Unlike the body proper, our spirit has access to energies and assistance not available through the only-physical dimension. It can open to the guidance, divine forces, and healing energies required for good health and success.

When our spirit is expressed fully through our body, a lot of seemingly impossible things become possible. Even physical miracles are possible, because our spirit, expressing its purpose in the world, has divine permission to shift or change our physical body if this will make it easier for us to accomplish our spiritual mission.

## What are the physical (normal) factors that determine my possible health?

These are the real, or measurable, factors that determine our optimum health:

- Genes

- Epigenetics (see chapter 8)

- Family system background

- Ability to heal and manage emotions (discussed later in this chapter)

- Mental capacity and issues (discussed later in this chapter)

- Attitude and happiness quotient (discussed later in this chapter)

- Spiritual beliefs (discussed later in this chapter)

- Lifestyle choices, such as diet, exercise, and time spent learning, at leisure, working, relating, and contemplating

There are many wellness-based approaches to creating transformation in these listed areas. Allopathic methods include surgery, drugs, medicine, diet, and exercise. Holistic processes include using herbs, addressing emotions and beliefs, and employing energy medicine. There are also integrative practices available that put these two processes together. Energy medicine is one such process. Energy medicine practitioners see diseases as energetic imbalances. They then use the energy in substances, thoughts, actions, and spirit to balance the distorted energy to create more wholeness. While energy medicine and spiritual practices can often result in dramatic and miraculous shifts, these usually follow the long, slow methods of becoming healthier.

## Can't I just have a miracle instead of doing the work?

Sometimes you can. Recently, I prayed with a client who had four major problems in his life, including a health care issue and a financial problem. We asked the Divine to intervene, and within an hour, I received an e-mail. Every negative condition had disappeared, and his fortunes had suddenly turned from bad to good. I happen to know, however, that this client had spent years "working on his issues"—code for examining his past for problems and changing his behavior to reflect his true self.

It is more likely that better physical health will follow effort on our part. For instance, I once worked with a woman who was overweight, topping the scale at over three hundred pounds. She had heard that I worked with food issues and that sometimes people lost a great deal of weight in a short amount of time. This particular client was looking for a metaphysical cure in order to achieve good health, and she wanted it NOW.

She was surprised and angry when I informed her that, given the clairvoyant insights I received, I could not dispense weight loss instantly. She was going to have to change her eating habits and exercise.

"Why can't you just make me lose weight?" my client asked.

I explained that there were a number of supporting activities we could conduct, including using guided visualization for her to establish her goals, perhaps a past life regression to unlock deeper issues, and evaluating her food choices based on her chakra type. She was interested in the last, and I referred her to my book *Attracting Your Perfect Body Through the Chakras*, which helps people test their chakra types and "feed" these appropriately, with the correct foods, exercise program, and thoughts. When I explained that all these methods would still take time, my client rebelled: "I don't want to work on it."

I asked her to return when she was willing to put energy into herself so that she could take the extra fat off her body.

## How can I receive a physical healing or change through spiritual means?

Sometimes our bodies transform into a more optimum state because our true self, or spirit, assists us. Occasionally, this occurs in a miraculous way. I remember working with a woman with severe arthritis. The pictures suggested that she held anger inside of her muscles, and that the resulting inflammation was creating the conditions for her problems. As she meditated on this information, I suggested that she ask the Divine for a healing.

She was suddenly filled with a sense of forgiveness— forgiveness for self and for others. A voice spoke to her, suggesting that there wasn't even a real reason for this forgiveness. She had always been loved and still was. The arthritis completely disappeared from her body.

Sometimes, our spirit—and the Great Spirit—provides miracles in unexpected ways. Yes, an energy healing can affect a "cure," a reversal of symptoms or the sudden creation of a never-before-realized physical level of perfection. Most often, however, it does not.

Instead, we receive miracles a different way, such as in the meeting of a new friend, an altered attitude, a sudden surge of love, or a willingness to undergo change. Because of this, I often caution clients against "predefining" the desired outcome. Instead, ask—and be grateful for what is received.

Once, I had a client with a genetic disease. In layman's terms, it was called a bone-breaking disease. If the slightest pressure was put on any of her bones, they would break. As you can imagine, this condition had significantly inhibited her activities throughout her life, and continued to do so. She was single, overweight, and unhappy when she came to me asking for a healing.

My client wanted a physical cure: a complete, idealized, instant cure. The images I received did not warrant an assurance of this cure. Instead, I saw a picture of a Thanksgiving turkey that, when carved, burst into fireworks. From this, I drew the conclusion that my client needed to count her blessings, and if she could do so, a surprise might follow.

My client was not very happy about this picture and interpretation, but she decided to play along. I passed her paper and pen and asked her to list everything she was grateful for; my clairvoyance provided a few of the pictures. She was thankful for her dog and her friends, her ability to deal with tough situations, the spring air and the flowers she grew when the climate changed from winter to warmth. As she connected with these loving thoughts, she began to sense a tingling throughout her body. She turned violently red, and I felt scared. Was she having a heart attack? A nervous breakdown? I was preparing to call a doctor when my client interrupted my thoughts.

"No, no," she gasped. "I'm okay. In fact, for the first time, I feel GREAT."

As my client reported in a subsequent session, she had not experienced a cure. Her bone-breaking disease did not disappear. Rather, her spine began to straighten. This enabled her to walk with more grace and ease. She was able to begin the exercise program that had previously been impossible. She lost weight and was stimulated to eat in a healthier way. Looking and feeling better about herself, she began to dress with more care, and she met a man—someone she really liked, who, by the way, she is now married to.

We cannot control what our own spirit might or might not do, but we can be open to the miraculousness that is all of life.

## How do I know if a physical condition will heal or not?

You do not know if it can be cured. Addressing the issues creating the problem, however, will invite a healing, whether it is physical, emotional, mental, or spiritual.

## How do I know what to do to increase my chances of a physical cure?

Use your own intuition. Intuition links you with the Divine, as well as with your own spirit. Review the material about spiritual gifts in chapter 8 and determine which gifts are your strongest. Now use that gift to ask for insight from the Divine. Here is an outline of how to do this.

*If you have first-chakra gifts:*

Seek a physical sign. Check inside of your body to determine what actions make it feel better. First-chakra people respond best to physical treatments.

*If you have second-chakra gifts:*

Focus on your feelings. What activities, treatments, or healing modalities, upon reflection, make you feel happier? Look for and deal with any repressed emotions or feelings.

*If you have third-chakra gifts:*

Review your thoughts and beliefs. Ask the Divine to send you information that will help you decide the best course of action.

*If you have fourth-chakra gifts:*

Examine your relationships; this is where you receive information and healing. Seek out trusted people or spiritual guides for insight.

*If you have fifth-chakra gifts:*

Ask for messages to come through verbal communiqués from people you know, the radio, music, and spiritual guides.

*If you have sixth-chakra gifts:*

Vision is your medium. You might literally read a message on a billboard, or you might receive the images on your mind-screen, as I do.

*If you have seventh-chakra gifts:*

Contemplate the Divine. As a spiritual person, your intuition is most accessible when you pray or meditate.

*If you have eighth-chakra gifts:*

Communication from the spirit world is your talent. Messages from entities, energies, angels, and deceased souls are available to you as long as you are open to receiving them.

*If you have ninth-chakra gifts:*

Look to your ideals. Your sense of higher principle and knowledge of the right thing to do will direct you every time.

*If you have tenth-chakra gifts:*

Communion with nature is the ability you can use to receive information. Birds, animals, trees, forces of nature—all of these can provide omens and signs of what to do. Consider the path of the most natural healing techniques, as you are an environmentally sensitive person.

*If you have eleventh-chakra gifts:*

Command change. Use your leadership skills and demand help when and where you need it.

*If you have twelfth-chakra gifts:*

You have your own unique way of knowing. Draw it forth and believe what you hear, see, sense, or know.

## Can beings from the spirit world help my physical well-being?

Absolutely. Many spirits, including deceased loved ones, angels, nature beings, and the Divine, pursue their spiritual mission by tending to the living. For some, this includes providing healing, occasionally physical healing.

Sometimes the guides actually prevent a physical disaster. I worked with an elderly gentleman who reported that just days before, he had been crossing the street when a car suddenly sped toward him. He felt winged beings lift him up and fly him curbside just as the car was about to hit him. Angels saved his life.

Another client talked about praying to the Divine in the form of the Divine Mother. Her daughter was ill— seriously ill, in fact, and was expected to die within hours.

My client felt a sudden breeze enter the room and heard the call of a robin, even though it was the dead of winter. Her daughter suddenly raised her head, coughed, and began to rise. She was completely cured.

For my part, I always pray to the Divine, to Christ, to help me with my healing work. I like to go straight to the top, as there are many entities and energies that would rather hurt than help people. This way, the Divine appoints the correct "medic" and I can trust who or what will show up.

I once worked with a client with severe acne. The poor boy's face was literally covered with scars and pustules. The spirit that appeared after my prayer was an ancient Chinese doctor, who "squirted" some sort of energetic herbal concoction all over my client's face. The boy's face began to sting and turn red. Within a few days, he called; his face was clear. Even the scars had disappeared.

Some guides simply accompany a client through life's ups—as well as through life's downs. I worked with one little boy who eventually died, but as he explained, he was not scared. He had a wolf that walked with him everywhere. Whenever he had pain, the wolf would breathe into his face and the pain would dissipate. The boy's mother told me that just before her son died, he sat up in bed and said, "It's okay, Mom, Wolf is here." He then slipped into a coma with a peaceful look on his face, dying later that day.

## What do you think is the cause of most physical diseases?

I believe that up to 80 percent of all physical illnesses and problems are caused by others' energies.

It is not that other people want to hurt us specifically. Physical reality is based on subtle reality. Subtle reality has no boundaries. It can bend, shape, ignore, or even create energy that can cause the physical world to conform to a set of higher standards.

Some subtle or psychic energies are positive and life enhancing, such as good thoughts and loving actions. Others are negative and can cause great harm. I once demonstrated the power of negative energies when teaching a class with one hundred people in it, bringing a woman to the stage and using kinesiology to make my point.

Kinesiology tests muscular strength. If someone is composed and exposed to supportive energies, his or her muscles remain strong. If tugged on, an outstretched arm holds firm. When vulnerable to a compromising element, the person loses muscular strength. When pulled on, the outstretched arm can be forced downward.

During this exercise, I asked 98 of the 99 onlookers to send my "guinea pig" positive thoughts. The other person? I requested that he think mean thoughts. His negative thoughts were loud enough to overpower the happy ones, and the student in front immediately lost muscle strength.

Others' negative energies can make us sick. They can create bad feelings, disastrous thoughts, and low self-esteem. They can convince us that the Divine does not love us. These negative energies can make us set goals that don't suit us and prevent us from using the spiritual gifts innate to us. They aren't really more powerful than positive energies, but they are literally lower in vibration. That's why they seem so powerful—we tend to pay more attention to what creates the biggest impact.

These destructive energies can originate from the people around us and also from spirits and entities. They can also emanate from people who do not live close to us, even people on the other side of the world. Energy has no boundaries and can transfer immediately.

## What makes me vulnerable to negative energies?

We often become susceptible to detrimental energies when we are young. Different psychic energies enter different chakras, based on frequency and intention. Physical energies, for instance, are registered in the first chakra. Through this chakra, we might take in an illness from a parent, especially if that parent does not want to deal with the problem.

Psychic energy can transform into physical matter through our chakras. Thus our parent's cold can suddenly show up in our own body. Worse, a parent's cancer might do the same.

In general, the easiest way to evaluate which chakra is absorbing energies that aren't your own is to pay attention to the chakra locations and the issues each demonstrate. The following chart will help you do this:

| Chakra | Physiological Touchstones |
|---|---|
| One: genital area | Genital organs and adrenals; coccygeal vertebrae; affects some kidney, bladder, and excrement functions; skin |
| Two: abdominal area | Affects part of adrenal endocrine system; intestines; parts of kidney function; some aspects of reproductive system; sacral vertebrae and the neurotransmitters determining emotional responses to stimuli |
| Three: solar plexus | Pancreas endocrine system; all digestive organs in stomach area, including liver, spleen, gallbladder, stomach, pancreas, and parts of kidney system; lumbar vertebrae |
| Four: heart | Heart and lungs; circulatory and oxygenation systems; breasts; lumbar and thoracic vertebrae |
| Five: throat | Thyroid endocrine gland; larynx; mouth and auditory systems; lymph system; thoracic vertebrae |
| Six: forehead | Pituitary endocrine gland; parts of hypothalamus; visual and olfactory systems; memory storage; some problems with ears and sinus; left eye |

| Seven:<br>top of the head | Pineal endocrine gland;<br>parts of hypothalamus;<br>higher learning and<br>cognitive brain systems;<br>parts of immune system |
|---|---|
| Eight:<br>1 inch above the head | Thymus (immune system);<br>memory retrieval functions;<br>aspects of central nervous<br>system; thalamus; right eye |
| Nine:<br>1 foot above the head | Diaphragm; pineal gland;<br>corpus callosum and<br>other higher learning<br>centers, including the<br>cortex and neocortex |
| Ten:<br>1½ feet underground | Feet, legs, and bones |
| Eleven:<br>around the body, especially<br>the hands and feet | Parts of skin, muscles,<br>and connective tissue |
| Twelve:<br>in 32 points on body;<br>connected to energetic egg | Secondary chakric sites:<br>includes the knees, elbows,<br>palms, and organs; this layer<br>connects to your energy egg |

## If you had one piece of advice to give me in relation to physical health, what would it be?

Make wholesome choices in all areas of your life.

# Emotional and Mental Health

## What is the definition of emotional health?

We are emotionally healthy when we are able to connect with and appropriately express our feelings. There are no good or bad feelings, only the positive or negative uses of them.

## What are feelings?

Feelings are the messengers of the body. They tell us what is happening inside of our bodies and link our soul to physical reality.

Regardless of how many types of feelings we are familiar with, there are only five feeling constellations, or groups of feelings. Each of these informs us of what is going on inside and outside of us.

**Anger:** Suggests that something or someone has violated our boundaries and we need to establish better protection.

**Fear:** Reveals that something or someone is endangering us and we must move forward, backward, or sidewise.

**Sadness:** Highlights that we have lost something or someone important to us; insinuates that we are not seeing the healing power of love in the situation.

**Happiness:** States that we want more of what we are experiencing.

**Disgust:** Insists that whatever or whomever we are in contact with is bad for us, and we must immediately distance ourselves.

Notice how each of these feelings provides practical instruction? In my work, I always search for the feelings underneath a presenting problem—a problem of any sort—to evaluate whether the client has a feeling that could offer advice, even if it is repressed or ignored.

## Is an emotion the same as a feeling?

An emotion is a thought plus a feeling. Usually thoughts or beliefs float around our minds and systems independent of feelings. They marry when the situation requires a quick response, such as when we are in life-threatening danger.

Imagine that a train is rushing at you, and your shoelace is stuck in the track. Not a good scene. What happens? The thought that "trains are dangerous" conjoins with the feeling of fear, forming an emotion that bursts forth as adrenaline. You think quickly, lose the shoe, and jump off the track.

Our bodies are designed to disconnect the belief and the feeling when a situation has finished—as in, when the train has passed, leaving you safe—but this does not always happen. Maybe you had a negative experience on a train as a child or during a past life, and the near-accident solidified the emotion. You unconsciously decided to permanently wed the thought that "trains are dangerous" with fear. The problem is that every time you look at a train, even a child's play toy, you become terrified.

These times of emotional binding cause strangleholds that can severely limit our happiness and health. An emotion creating fear of trains is one thing. What about a terror of doctors? Of men or women? Of work? The anchoring belief traps the feeling inside the body, and over time, these stuck feelings can result in even more serious conditions, such as illness.

### How do you as a clairvoyant diagnose problematic emotions or feelings?

I am able to visualize the following for my clients:

- Stuck or repressed feelings
- Dysfunctional thoughts
- Stuck emotions
- Others' feelings, thoughts, or emotions
- "Missing" feelings, thoughts, or emotions
- Depression and anxiety

I psychically see stuck or repressed feelings as muddy, brackish, or "off" colors that puddle somewhere in or around a person's energy system or body. Cancer, for instance, shows up as three different ugly colors. Depending on the color, I can make a metaphysical diagnosis of the type of cancer and suggest the energetic solutions. I will demonstrate what I mean by analyzing one type of cancer, as this process reveals the same routine I go through for nearly every issue.

A darkish blue or black-shaded energy indicates that the cancer might be caused by physical toxins and perhaps stuck emotions. If this image appears, I ask questions of the Divine to further clarify the situation. What is the source of the physical toxicity? When did this infestation occur? Was it recently or in the past? I once asked these questions for a client with serious breast cancer and saw a picture of a pencil with a date imprinted on it: 1964. I asked if she had ever been exposed to lead paint in childhood and she said yes, at her childhood farmhouse. She was born in 1964.

I next ask questions about the feelings. Are there stuck feelings? Are they others' feelings that have been absorbed and are therefore unable to be processed by this person? Or are there perhaps "missing" feelings, feelings that should have been felt during a traumatic or challenging experience but were instead shoved outside of the body because they were considered too frightening to feel?

I am able to feel other peoples' feelings, so I am usually able to sense what is stuck. I will psychically perceive a blank spot where there ought to be a feeling and a long, garden-hose-type of cord leading to the disenfranchised feeling. I follow the cord and find the feeling that has been missing. Others' feelings look like big, bulging tumors, growths that don't fit in the person's energy system. Many, many problems—including cancers, heart disease, and emotional and mental health illnesses—start from the absorption of others' feelings.

I once worked with a woman with sarcoma in her abdomen. I perceived a bulging mass of red energy in the middle of the tumor and asked her if anyone had ever hit her when she was growing up. Red often indicates the presence of anger. She replied yes, her brother used to beat her up. His favorite spot for abusing her? Her belly. We asked the Divine to release her brother's energy, which had transferred from him to her every time he struck her. As soon as the brother's energy left, my client began to cry. She called me days later and said that she had been grieving. The next time she went in for a health check, it was discovered that the mass had lost its malignancy.

My final evaluation in a clairvoyant diagnosis is made to pinpoint the thoughts that might compose an emotional issue. To do this, I literally ask to talk with these thoughts. Sometimes they jump out of the cancerous growth looking like real people. And sometimes, they are—except they might be entities or energies that have invaded the person and are causing the cancer. Other times, the emerging beings are representative of the person who gave negative messages to the cancer patient. In one case, a man's mother appeared in a white apron, holding a great big wooden spoon. At first, I thought *how sweet, a mom who cooks*. But no, she began to whack my client with a spoon. It turns out that she was a stay-at-home mother who hated being at home. She would verbally berate her son for having been born, therefore ruining her career. My client had decided that his life was not worth living. Although his cancer did not disappear, releasing this stream of negative thought provided him serenity with his dying process.

## How do you detect depression and anxiety?

There are many clairvoyant signs for depression and anxiety. In general, depression will look like a square somewhere in the body, and it will contain the issue that is causing the depression. I worked with a woman who had been depressed since childhood. Upon examining the black box in her ovaries, we determined that her mother had tried to abort her. Once she relived the horror of this in-womb experience and invited in the Divine Mother's love, the depression cleared up.

Anxiety looks like a spiral or circle that is out of control. This symbol always points to a fear that we have about the future. I help clients track these spirals so we can bust the fear open and discover its cause. For instance, one anxious client was scared about money. She was sure that she would end up broke and destitute at the end of her life. I asked her to imagine the source of this fear, and she saw her father, who had died in an alcoholic stupor alone and poor. We asked the Divine to send healing to his soul, and my client was immediately relieved of her own anxiety.

## Can thoughts really make me sick?

Absolutely. Our mind runs our body, and our thoughts run our mind.

There is actually a scientific fact called the nocebo effect. The placebo effect, its twin, works by convincing our mind that a neutral substance can produce a healing effect. The nocebo does the opposite. It persuades our mind that a neutral material can make us sick. Thoughts operate our bodies—as well as the world.

## What does happiness have to do with physical well-being?

The studies are in; the ayes have it. Happier people are healthier. They recover faster from illness or surgery. And they have more friends—another reason that they are happier.

A few of the original meanings of the word *happy* are "lucky" and "fortunate." *Whole* derives from words meaning "healthy," "sacred," and "welfare." Knowing that we are already whole, no matter our physical state, makes us feel fortunate. Believing ourselves lucky or full of fortune will better our welfare. Seeing our bodies as holy and the physical world as sacred accomplishes both goals.

How would you live if you really understood that your body was sacred? A happy person is more apt to be devoted—to be full of love—toward his or her body than an unhappy person.

I once worked with a woman who was diagnosed with fourth-stage cancer. The doctors refused even to treat her, because her body was riddled with tumors. They suggested that she go home and prepare to die. She came to see me instead.

This woman did not look particularly healthy—she was overweight and didn't dress very carefully—but she didn't look close to death, either. I asked if she had gotten a second opinion. She said yes, she had consulted doctors at the famous Mayo Clinic, the University of Minnesota, and elsewhere. She was set to die.

I heard a voice in my head, which I believed to be the Divine, which had another question for her:

"Well, are you willing to be happy anyway?"

She blinked, obviously surprised by the question, and then answered with a yes.

We did not talk about her illness or potential treatments or the traumas of dying. I did suggest that she update her will, because it is always smart to do that. We talked at length about everything she wanted to do with her life. She loved to crochet. She loved to bake. And she liked working. I suggested she continue these activities and enjoy herself.

She returned four years later. She was still overweight and wasn't dressed any more carefully, but there she was— alive. She said she had been enjoying her life but had started to get a few pains in her abdomen, and because of that she had revisited the doctors. They had taken x-rays and were astonished that she was still alive; her body was still replete with cancer. I asked my client what she wanted to do with our session, and she said that since the last prescription for happiness had worked so well, she figured she needed to update it in order to live a few more years. We reviewed her activities and added a couple more. It has now been another year, and her daughter-in-law, who recently came for a session, informed me that my "cancer-infested" client is doing fine.

## If there is one thing I should remember about my feelings and thoughts, what might it be?

Feelings and thoughts are positive. They help us negotiate reality. They only become problems when they merge into emotions and make us stuck. If you are having chronic difficulties, check for emotional stuckness—for a feeling that has become permanently paired with a belief. Remember the situation that formed the emotion in the first place and then rethink your conclusions. This will free the feeling from the thought and you from the past.

# Spiritual Health

## Why has my life been so hard?

This is such an important question, and most of us think it even if we don't ask it aloud. Most of us feel that life is really difficult—something to endure rather than enjoy.

Part of the reason is that life *is* hard. On this planet, we have free will. Collectively, humanity has decided, through thousands of years of evolution and experience, to establish a set of rules that make life hard. We have unconsciously accepted greed, evil, cruelty, and other detrimental forces as dominant and actually cultivated violence and abuse.

We are all products of this group consciousness.

For solace, many of us turn to addictive behavior, abusing others or ourselves in an attempt to numb the pain and avoid self-responsibility. The truth is that the real hardship of life is making personal choices from integrity and love rather than programmed desires and shame. Few of us like to stand out in a crowd, and so we go along with the group mind.

## Is life hard because I keep doing things wrong?

Most of us blame ourselves for life's problems. While we are responsible for our decisions, we are not responsible for the way the world is.

Most of us think that when things go wrong, there is something wrong with us because of our spiritual beliefs.

The three major world religions insist that we are victims of original sin. A long time ago, our forebears made a huge mistake, and we are doomed to do the same, forever and ever. From the start, it appears we don't have a chance.

We do inherit and copy patterns from our parents, and their parents, and so on. But we are not inherently evil or sinful. Rather, we are all affected by and contained within a negative group mindset that makes us feel bad about ourselves. Within this mesh—or mess—we have free will, however. We can use our intuition to break away and live freely.

The second dominant philosophy is often termed New Age, or spiritual. It has been most recently proposed in the book and movie *The Secret*, and it asserts that what we think becomes what we get. If people are mean to us, it is because we have to examine the meanness in ourselves.

This value set establishes a standard of perfection that is impossible to achieve. It is also at least partially inaccurate. We are not responsible for what others do or say. We do not cause their reactions, even to us; therefore, we don't cause what everything else in life is doing around—or to—us.

Instead of blaming ourselves, we need to take responsibility for ourselves and then let the rest go—and know that half of what life hands or shows us will ask us to say no. Life shows us what *not* to do as often as it shows us *what* to do.

## Why have I made so many mistakes?

It is easy to live backwards, berating ourselves with comments like "I should have" or "I might have" or "I didn't." We learn by experience. A mistake is only a mistake if we keep making the same one.

Going forward, walking into tomorrow from today, why not try something new? Instead of evaluating choices based on the belief that there is something wrong with you, try believing yourself whole.

## The world seems especially hard right now. How can I deal with it?

Life does seem especially challenging right now, although I would argue that many generations have made the same claim. Worldwide, our contemporary society is being barraged by emotional despair, financial downturns, chaotic confusion, galloping unemployment, and toxic pollution. What do I tell people to do? This is what I am doing with my clients.

> **Informing:** Individuals, organizations, and countries go through seven- to ten-year growth cycles. A "downturn" is the perfect time to recalibrate, repurpose, and redesign. Let go of what didn't and doesn't work.

> **Warning:** We haven't stayed up to date. We've been overspending, underplanning, and filling in the margins—like scribbling in the blank sides of a paper—without letting go of what's

not working. Continuing this bad behavior will create more bad results.

**Pruning:** It's time to determine what should be discarded. Put a stop to what needs to stop so that you don't slip further down the rabbit hole.

**Separating:** It's *vital* to separate the self from the group mindset, the chaos that only creates fear and trepidation.

**Healing:** This is the time to address inner fears— anxiety and depression. Use the chaos to uncover and recover from problems already within. *Use* the negative energy, don't become it.

**Evaluating:** Companies and individuals have purposes and gifts. Becoming successful—even through loss—requires forming a clear picture and outline of specific gifts and abilities.

**Creating:** There are always opportunities. Pay attention, and you will see the holes of light in the darkness.

**Attracting:** Help others. Partner. Be grateful. Do this through attitude, energy, and a life-enhancing mindset.

**Holding faith:** This is the ideal time to ask the right questions—to admit powerlessness and begin (or continue) to rely on the Divine.

**Relying on intuition:** Maybe it is time to really commune with the Divine.

If there is a summary statement, it's this: *Come from heart, not mind.*

## How can I "see the light" when I'm confused?

Look into yourself.

Really.

We are made of light; it is a scientific fact. The entire universe is surrounded by and interpenetrated with a field of light. Our DNA and bodies are formed of light. Sound wraps everything together. (For more information, see my book *The Subtle Body*.)

I like to add that we are also made of shadows, memories of self and other that are incomplete in that they have not been brought to the light. We must meet our "selves" in the shadows and free them from the mists of shame and fear in order to live fully as the loving and light beings that we are. Our individual paths all include embracing the shadowland dreams that have never come true, to breathe them into reality.

## How do I know which god to pray to?

Before travel and the Internet, we were isolated. We grew up in families and communities that saw God a particular way. All Christians had the Bible—but each sect read it differently. Natives of the Kalahari had a version of the Divine—and their neighbors on the other side of Africa? They had their own ideas. We can now read, study, and evaluate each other's gods, and pick and choose the ideas that serve us.

If we are willing to use our brains to research and review intensively and to evaluate with our hearts, we can form ideals about the Divine that suit us—that awaken, enlighten, and embrace the best of human standards.

I follow Christ. When working with clients, I suggest that they ask the Divine which earthly version of him/her/it—if any—suits them. A client recently decided to work with Kuan Yin, an Oriental female goddess, as she embodied the principles that my client was striving for. I encourage all my clients to listen to their own hearts. I don't think that God cares what name we use for him/her, what worship site we visit, or what label we slap on ourselves. The Divine is love. There are many faces and forms of love, but they must all result in something good to be considered love.

## How can I manifest what I want?

You receive what you are able to dream into being. Partner with the Divine to ask for what you really want, not what you *think* you want. Do the hard work of reclaiming your past, of healing shame and fear. Be willing to work hard for what you truly desire. And know that all spiritually good things will help you on your way.

## Do I choose my time of death?

When we write our soul plan, we usually select several exit points, times that would be appropriate for us to die. I once worked with a healing teacher who knew that she was in such a time. She was deathly ill. She prayed for guidance and eventually decided to stay so she could write books. She almost immediately became well.

One of my most poignant professional moments involved a visit from a young nurse. She was only twenty-four years old. She didn't really want me to "check in"; she only asked me questions about death. She then said that she was going go send her mother and sister to see me in about a year, and that I was to tell them where she had left a letter hidden in her bedroom.

A year later, the mother and sister visited me. They told me that each had received a strange call from my original client a week ago, telling them to make an appointment the next week. They did. The original client was killed in an automobile accident a few days after the phone call. She was helping another motorist on the side of the road when a car hit her. Moments before, she had thrust the other individual out of the way.

Had my client predicted her own death? At one level, it sounded like she had. If only each of us were able to surrender so willingly in the final moments; having lived lives of love, we would then release ourselves into an even greater love.

# Conclusion

Like all of us, I was born special. My uniqueness would not have shown up on an intelligence test or made me any sort of prodigy. Nonetheless, I was extraordinary in that I could see what was out of the ordinary.

My gift has been painfully honed and shaped. While it provides me solace—the sight of the Divine—through times of hardship, it also sometimes makes my life difficult. I have not always enjoyed being different. My parents did not like my differences. And the church thought I was way too different.

Outwardly, I have lived a normal life despite my peculiarities. I married. I had a child. I divorced. I married again, had another child, and divorced again. I have studied and worked and made money and raised children and animals and cleaned the house, all the while pursuing my real interests: spirituality, healing, and intuition. These have become the tools of my business, the subjects of my books, and the reasons I travelled around the world to understand the invisible and the inaudible. I have really been looking for God—the God in nature, in books, in us all.

Have I found what I was searching for? I do, every day. I see the Divine in the eyes, hearts, and lives of every client who walks into my office or calls me on the phone.

I see evidence of divine love in the stories of my friends, children, and clients. I see God in stories on the news. I see God in the tears of the man who held his wife's hand as she died. I see God in the shaman who healed a child of cancer with plant medicine. I see God in the ambassador who died for peace in another country. I see God in the schoolteacher who gave up a multimillion-dollar career in sports to motivate kids toward greatness. I see God in the twenty-one-year-old young man who started an amazing business and now gives away money to needy causes.

The Divine is present in everything. My oldest son, Michael, was attuned to this when he was just a toddler. One day, he was sitting in his high chair eating spaghetti, when he turned to me and asked a question.

"Mommy, does Jesus like spaghetti?" I was surprised at the question.

"I guess so," I pondered. "Why?"

"Well, because Jesus is in my heart, and the spaghetti has to go through my heart to get to my stomach."

We each have special gifts and abilities. We are each here to be heroes—to live our purpose in an authentic way to self and others. We are each needed. We are each called to be who we really are and to help others, this planet, and ourselves evolve.

My heart hurts the most when I see people throwing their gifts away through addictions, denial, or simply lack of use.

The real question is, have you found what you are searching for? If there is one constant among people—the thousands I have met and been honored to work with—it would be that we are all searching. We seek. And we find. Then, we seek again. My hope is that in your travels, inward and outward, you know that you have all the special gifts and abilities you already need not only to conduct the honorable and heroic search but to live all your dreams, as well. We are all born with a purpose. We have been living on-purpose. The path can only become brighter and wider as we open to the ways of spirit.

YOUR VISION WILL become clear only when
you look into your heart. Who looks outside,
dreams. Who looks inside, awakens.

—Carl Gustav Jung

# Appendix

## The Gifts

### Chakra-Based Psychic Gifts:
### Shifting from Psychic to Intuitive

We are born with psychic gifts within each of our chakras. These can be used for positive reasons but can also cause disturbances and difficulties. We evolve these gifts by developing them consciously, at which point they become intuitive rather than psychic abilities. The following chart depicts the innate psychic gifts and their potential positive and negative affects, as well as the "grown-up" intuitive aptitudes.

| Chakra | Psychic Gift | Positive Psychic Ability |
|--------|--------------|--------------------------|
| First | Physical sympathy (a factor in psychometry, dowsing, psychic surgery, kinesiology, telekinesis, and hands-on healing) | Senses others' physical problems and the reasons for them |
| Second | Feeling sympathy | Feels others' feelings and can decipher them |
| Third | Mental sympathy (often called clairsentience) | Knows what others are thinking or believe |
| Fourth | Relational sympathy (a factor in hands-on healing) | Can sense others' needs and desires; can channel energy for healing |
| Fifth | Verbal sympathy (also called channeling, transmediumship, telepathy, and clairaudience) | Can receive data from another person or spirit, as well as tones, music, or sounds |
| Sixth | Visual sympathy (also called clairvoyance, futuring, precognition, use of "the Sight," remote viewing, reading the aura) | Sees images, visions, pictures, and colors with eyes or inner sight |

| Negative Psychic Ability | Intuitive Gift |
|---|---|
| Absorbs others' illnesses and physical conditions and cannot get rid of them | Physical empathy: registers others' physical conditions but releases them; can help heal them |
| Absorbs others' feelings and holds them in own body | Feeling empathy: reads others' emotions and can help heal them |
| Thinks that others' beliefs or thoughts are one's own | Mental empathy: determines belief-system causes of others' issues and provides clarification |
| Assumes responsibility for others' needs, unmet desires, and healing | Relational empathy: can determine others' needs and provide assistance, but invites divine help for the rest |
| Cannot separate own thoughts from those outside of self; can be overtaken by spirits | Verbal empathy: controls opening and shutting for receiving communication |
| No control over flow or type of images; often mainly negative; cannot interpret what is real | Visual empathy: receives revelation when needed, able to interpret; can heal others with visions |

| | | |
|---|---|---|
| Seventh | Spiritual sympathy (also called prophecy and a factor in intentionality, prayer, meditation) | Can sense consciousness development, purpose, destiny, or spiritual guides of others |
| Eighth | Shamanic sympathy (a factor in soul journeying, remote viewing, retrocognition, projection, precognition, the exorcism or summoning of spirits, and work with restrictions | Walks between worlds and dimensions; not boundaried by time—past, present, or future |
| Ninth | Soul sympathy | Can tell what is going on in others' souls |
| Tenth | Natural sympathy (a factor in nature-based healing) | Links with elements, beings, and energies of the natural world |
| Eleventh | Force sympathy | Conduit for natural and energetic forces, such as wind or spiritual beings |
| Twelfth | Personal aptitudes: manages special and unique abilities related to one's specific spiritual purpose— similar to the siddhi abilities discussed in chapter 8 on the chakras. | Differs from person to person but is an extension of personality traits. For example, if someone has a keen memory and is a teacher, this would involve psychic ability to "hear" data related to subject matter; this unfiltered process can expose the teacher to inaccurate or ineffective data. |

| | |
|---|---|
| Vulnerable to spiritual attacks, overly affected by evil or negativity, sense of powerlessness | Spiritual empathy: manages access to higher guides to help self or others; uses prayer, meditation, intention toward healing |
| Vulnerable to entities and issues from other worlds, people, and own past lives | Shamanic empathy: can connect to or visit other worlds and dimensions to obtain information or healing energy or conduct energy and entity shifts |
| Takes on others' soul issues or global problems | Soul empathy: senses others' soul needs or global needs and determines how to create harmony |
| Becomes a victim of natural elements, beings, and energies | Natural empathy: receives and can share information and healing energies from natural world |
| Run by outside forces, leading to extreme negativity or out-of-control power | Force empathy: can pick and choose which forces to use, tap into, and direct for positive change |
| Differs from person to person but always furthers directed use of the psychic for a higher purpose. Example: a teacher could decide to "receive" the psychic data to conduct a particular lesson. The intuitive process allows for control of subject matter (whereas the psychic does not). | Differs from person to person but always helps others achieve their spiritual purpose. For example, a teacher would "receive" only the psychic information that would meet the highest ends of his or her students. |

# The Evolving Gifts

After psychic ability transforms into the intuitive talent, we have a decision to make: to use our gifts to achieve our spiritual destiny or not. If we say yes, the intuitive talent transforms into the spiritual gift.

| *Chakra* | *Psychic Gift* |
| --- | --- |
| First | Physical sympathy |
| Second | Feeling sympathy |
| Third | Mental sympathy |
| Fourth | Relational sympathy |
| Fifth | Verbal sympathy |
| Sixth | Visual sympathy |
| Seventh | Spiritual sympathy |
| Eighth | Shadow sympathy |
| Ninth | Soul sympathy |
| Tenth | Environmental sympathy |
| Eleventh | Force sympathy |
| Twelfth | |

| Intuitive Ability | Spiritual Gift |
|---|---|
| Physical empathy | Manifesting |
| Feeling empathy | Compassion/creativity |
| Mental empathy | Administration |
| Relational empathy | Healing |
| Verbal empathy | Word of Knowledge |
| Visual empathy | Revelation |
| Spiritual empathy | Prophecy |
| Shadow empathy | Power shamanism |
| Soul empathy | Harmony |
| Environmental empathy | Natural healing |
| Force empathy | Transmutation |
| | Mastery |

# GET MORE AT LLEWELLYN.COM

Visit us online to browse hundreds of our books and decks, plus sign up to receive our e-newsletters and exclusive online offers.

- **Free tarot readings** • **Spell-a-Day** • **Moon phases**
- **Recipes, spells, and tips** • **Blogs** • **Encyclopedia**
- **Author interviews, articles, and upcoming events**

# GET SOCIAL WITH LLEWELLYN

**Find us on Facebook**
www.Facebook.com/LlewellynBooks

**Follow us on**

**Follow us on twitter**
www.Twitter.com/Llewellynbooks

# GET BOOKS AT LLEWELLYN

## LLEWELLYN ORDERING INFORMATION

 **Order online:** Visit our website at www.llewellyn.com to select your books and place an order on our secure server.

**Order by phone:**
- Call toll-free within the U.S. at 1-877-NEW-WRLD (1-877-639-9753)
- Call toll free within Canada at 1-866-NEW-WRLD (1-866-639-9753)
- We accept VISA, MasterCard, and American Express

**Order by mail:**
Send the full price of your order (MN residents add 6.875% sales tax) in U.S. funds, plus postage and handling to: Llewellyn Worldwide, 2143 Wooddale Drive Woodbury, MN 55125-2989

**POSTAGE AND HANDLING:**
STANDARD: (U.S., Mexico & Canada)
(Please allow 2 business days)
$25.00 and under, add $4.00.
$25.01 and over, FREE SHIPPING.

INTERNATIONAL ORDERS (airmail only):
$16.00 for one book, plus $3.00 for each additional book.

Visit us online for more shipping options. Prices subject to change.

## FREE CATALOG!

To order, call
1-877-
NEW-WRLD
ext. 8236
or visit our
website

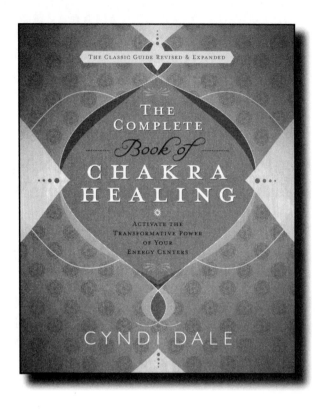

THE CLASSIC GUIDE REVISED & EXPANDED

# THE
# COMPLETE
## *Book of*
# CHAKRA
# HEALING

ACTIVATE THE
TRANSFORMATIVE POWER
OF YOUR
ENERGY CENTERS

CYNDI DALE

# The Complete Book of Chakra Healing

*Activate the Transformative Power of Your Energy Centers*

## Cyndi Dale

When first published in 1996 (as *New Chakra Healing*), Cyndi Dale's guide to the chakras established a new standard for healers, intuitives, and energy workers worldwide. This groundbreaking book quickly became a bestseller. It expanded the seven-chakra system to thirty-two chakras, explained spiritual points available for dynamic change, and outlined the energetic system so anyone could use it for health, prosperity, and happiness.

Presented here for the first time is the updated and expanded edition, now titled *The Complete Book of Chakra Healing*. With nearly 150 more pages than the original book, this groundbreaking edition is poised to become the next classic guide to the chakras. This volume presents a wealth of valuable new material:

- The latest scientific research explaining the subtle energy system and how it creates the physical world

- Depiction of the negative influences that cause disease, as well as ways to deal with them

- Explanations of two dozen energy bodies plus the meridians and their uses for healing and manifesting

978-0-7387-1502-5 • 7½ x 9⅛, 456 pp. • illus., charts, bibliog., index • $24.95

# The Street-Smart Psychic's Guide to Getting a Good Reading

**Lisa Barretta**

What's the secret to getting a fabulous psychic reading? Who better to ask than a professional psychic? Sassy, candid, and spot-on, Lisa Barretta's insider advice will bring you closer to the answers you seek. Half the battle is choosing a psychic. Learn how to avoid charlatans and select wisely among astrologers, mediums, tarot readers, psychic phone-line services, and others. True stories from Barretta's thirty-year career as a psychic will have you laughing as you learn what to do—and not do—to build a productive rapport with your reader. Maybe you'll even recognize yourself in her entertaining descriptions of "seeker types," such as the all-too-common "psychic junkie."

This unique guide also explores the fascinating life of a psychic, the pros and cons of psychic hotlines, and seeker/psychic etiquette.

**978-0-7387-1850-7 • 6 x 9, 312 pp. • $16.95**

A COMPLETE
PHYSICAL & SPIRITUAL GUIDE TO
HEALING YOUR CHRONIC PAIN

*Why We Hurt*

*Your Total Self-Care Guide for*
BACKACHES, HEADACHES,
SHOULDER PAIN, ARTHRITIS
*and*
FIBROMYALGIA

DR. GREG FORS
FOUNDER OF FENIX RECOVERY ENTERPRISES

# Why We Hurt

*A Complete Physical & Spiritual Guide
to Healing Your Chronic Pain*

## Dr. Greg Fors

More than 100 million Americans suffer from headaches, neck pain, backache, sciatica, arthritis, fibromyalgia, and other forms of chronic pain. Neurologist Greg Fors was among them until he created a comprehensive and compelling program for wellness based on the body-mind-spirit connection.

*Why We Hurt* is a practical guide and true lifelong companion to health and well-being that will inspire you to heal your pain. Understand the beneficial side of pain—the body's alarm system—and how it's linked to your thoughts, emotions, diet, lifestyle, and environment. Dr. Fors will guide you away from pain-masking drugs and other quick fixes and help you pinpoint the root cause of your pain. Best of all, he offers simple, effective strategies for overcoming pain—involving nutrition, spiritual/emotional balance, vitamin/herbal supplements, comprehensive trigger point therapy, and detoxification—to find your way back to wholeness and happiness. Also featured is a unique five-step program for spiritual and emotional healing based on the perennial wisdom of great philosophers and spiritual leaders.

978-0-7387-1065-5 • 7½ x 9⅛, 432 pp. • charts, illus.,
bibliog., resources, index • $24.95

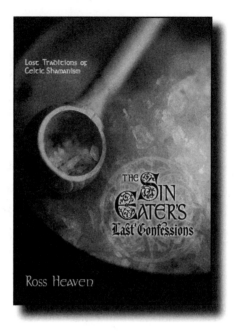

Lost Traditions of
Celtic Shamanism

THE **SIN EATER'S**
*Last Confessions*

ROSS HEAVEN

# The Sin Eater's Last Confessions
*Lost Traditions of Celtic Shamanism*

## Ross Heaven

Considered a madman in his English village, Adam Dilwyn Vaughan—a sin eater—was shunned by the same community who flocked to him for healing. This true tale records Ross Heaven's fascinating journey as the sin eater's apprentice, who is introduced to the lost art of sin eating and other Celtic shamanic traditions.

This spiritual memoir records the author's wondrous, moving experiences with the powerful energies of the natural world. He witnesses Adam removing negative energies from a patient, discovers his soul purpose through dreaming, goes on a vision quest in a sacred cave, and participates in a sin-eating ritual. Interlacing these remarkable events are Welsh legends and enlightening discussions that shed light on these mysterious practices and invite you to see the world through the eyes of a shaman. Also included is a sin eater's workbook of the same shamanic exercises and techniques practiced by Adam.

978-0-7387-1356-4 • 5 x 7, 288 pp. • bibliog., index • $16.95

## To Write to the Author

If you wish to contact the author or would like more information about this book, please write to the author in care of Llewellyn Worldwide and we will forward your request. Both the author and the publisher appreciate hearing from you and learning of your enjoyment of this book and how it has helped you. Llewellyn Worldwide cannot guarantee that every letter written to the author can be answered, but all will be forwarded. Please write to:

Cyndi Dale
ᶜ/o Llewellyn Worldwide
2143 Wooddale Drive
Woodbury, MN 55125-2989
Please enclose a self-addressed stamped envelope for reply,
or $1.00 to cover costs. If outside U.S.A., enclose
international postal reply coupon.

Many of Llewellyn's authors have websites with additional information and resources. For more information, please visit our website:

### http://www.llewellyn.com